D1599005

Revealing Antiquity

· 9 ·

G. W. Bowersock, General Editor

THE CRAFT OF ZEUS

Myths of Weaving and Fabric

JOHN SCHEID *&* JESPER SVENBRO

Translated by Carol Volk

HARVARD UNIVERSITY PRESS
CAMBRIDGE, MASSACHUSETTS
LONDON, ENGLAND
1996

Originally published in 1994 by Editions La Découverte as *Le métier
de Zeus: Mythe du tissage et du tissu dans le monde gréco-romain*

Library of Congress Cataloging-in-Publication Data
Scheid, John.
[Métier de Zeus. English]
The craft of Zeus : myths of weaving and fabric / John Scheid
and Jesper Svenbro : translated by Carol Volk.
p.   cm. — (Revealing antiquity : 9)
Includes bibliographical references and index.
ISBN 0-674-17549-2 (alk. paper)
1. Classical literature—-History and criticism.   2. Weaving in
literature.   3. Mythology, Classical, in literature.   4. Zeus (Greek
deity) in literature.   5. Civilization, Classical.   6. Weaving—
Greece.   7. Weaving—Rome.   I. Svenbro, Jesper, 1944–   .
II. Title.   III. Series.
PA3015.W48S34   1996
880.9'355—dc20
95-35699
CIP

ACKNOWLEDGMENTS

WE WISH TO THANK all those who helped and encouraged us by participating in our seminars at the Ecole Pratique des Hautes Etudes (section V) from 1985 to 1988. Part of Chapter 6 was presented at the round table "Paroles romaines" in Pont-à-Mousson in October 1991; Chapter 3 was presented at the seminar of Pierre Vidal-Naquet in January 1993. We thank all those who shared their observations with us on these occasions. We also thank the friends and colleagues who read the successive manuscripts of our work-in-progress, in particular Philippe Borgeaud, Claude Calame, Marcel Detienne, Françoise Frontisi, Stella Georgoudi, François Lissarrague, Philippe Moreau, Jean-Pierre Vernant, and Peter J. Wilson.

CONTENTS

CONTENTS

THE CRAFT OF ZEUS

INTRODUCTION

IN THE RESEARCH from which this book emerged, we confronted three challenges. First, although we began with a single metaphor, that of weaving and fabric,[1] we did not limit ourselves to exploring its application in a single field. On the contrary, it was by studying this metaphor in its various applications that we hoped to identify the areas in which its usage was most concrete. Rather than consider the metaphorical use of weaving solely in the case of poetic "weaving," for example, as one of us had already done,[2] it seemed important to examine its other uses, beginning with that of conjugal "weaving." And indeed, it soon became clear to us that marriage was an important, if not the most important, area of application, with political thought a third.[3] Thus the research for this book developed in the reverse order of the journey proposed for the reader: here the first section is devoted to political weaving, the second to conjugal weaving, and the third to poetic weaving.

Second, after a comparativist essay in 1985 contrasting the stories of the foundation of Carthage in Greek and Roman cultures,[4] we undertook a comparative study of the metaphor of weaving, juxtaposing Greek and Roman cultures in order to detect areas of similarity, difference, or even rupture. This comparativist approach informs all three sections. For three years, mainly during our "Religions of Rome" seminars at the Ecole Pratique des Hautes Etudes in Paris, we pursued this joint research, employing our respective capacities as a Hellenist and a Latinist,[5] using resemblances only as points of departure for critical reflection and taking care to study the elements sufficiently in context before drawing any comparisons.[6]

The third challenge is spelled out in the book's subtitle. Our choice of the word "myth," in preference to the more usual "metaphor," reflects the fact that the metaphor of weaving and fabric is a shared one—part of what is usually referred to as "common knowledge"—and not an individual creation. It is a figure of thought used by an entire civilization, repeated, modified, and resurrected over time without ever becoming fixed or dead. In our view this *shared* or common aspect justifies our use of the word "myth."

From the point of view that equates "myth" with "story," we acknowledge that things are a bit trickier. The difficulties encountered by mythology (in the usual sense of the word), iconology, and the study of rituals, when each, for the needs of its own interpretative work, makes use of the other two, are well known. These problems result in part from the fact that none of the three can claim a privileged position with respect to the other two: the story does not automatically hold the key to the image or the ritual, for example. Whether we are dealing with stories, images, or rituals, specific rules correspond to each field, requiring more cautious methods on the part of the scholar than mere juxtaposition or naive identification.

Moreover, mythology (still in the usual sense of the word) cannot be confined to the domain of stories: the pieces of information it employs in its analyses come from sources that are too varied to permit us to subscribe to an absolute hegemony of the narrative.

In reflecting upon these difficulties we came to consider the myth not as a story but as a simple linking or *concatenation of categories*, linking thanks to which it becomes possible, within a given culture, to engender mythical stories, images, and rituals.[7] Thus envisioned, the now-equal relationship among story, image, and ritual is one not of mirroring but of common descent, giving the respective documents an air of close parentage, the origin of which would be this linking of categories we call myth. In a given culture, this myth tends to remain relatively stable, and this stability is particularly evident when it is linguistic in nature.[8]

If, on the other hand, the association of the categories of, say, *fabric* and *city* is not linguistic in nature, it nonetheless seems to us as stable as if it had a basis in language, for the myth it created followed Greco-Roman civilization from its beginning to its end. An expression such as "the fabric of the city" (or "the city is a fabric") summarizes this myth, which is merely a kind of commonly shared *idée fixe* by means of which the members of a culture constantly try to explore and organize reality. In other words myth, in a given culture, is a simple "proposition," generating stories, images, rituals—and exegesis. Such a definition could in fact be based on the Greek word *muthos* itself, which means "story" of course, but primarily "word" or "proposition," as Roland Barthes once reminded us.[9]

In an article that served us as a theoretical guidepost, Marcel Detienne showed how the myth of the olive tree functioned in Attica:[10] like fabric, the olive tree furnishes a way to conceive of the city—though in a different fashion (with a different emphasis). Planted at set distances, olive trees are citizen-warriors rooted in the Attic soil. Similarly, ships and cattle are employed metaphorically—or, if one prefers, "mythically." Complementing one another, each provides a particular way to conceive of the city and forms an apparatus that politics needs to survive. In our view it is through these figures that political thought was invented.[11] Thus it is hardly a coincidence that these four myths—in the sense in which we are using the word here—are present at the greatest festival celebrating the political unity of Athens: the Panathenaea.

The perspective we are proposing is thus one of *generative* rather than "narrative" mythology, but we should add right away that this book is not primarily theoretical. We did not implement a predetermined theory, although in the course of our research we naturally had to grapple with problems of a theoretical nature.

Neither is this a book of iconology, in contrast to most previous research into weaving and fabric, from the major text by Margherita Guarducci published in the 1920s to the recent article by Jean-Marc Moret.[12] Aside from the fact that we are not specialists in figurative art, we were interested chiefly in seeking the meaning of the metaphor of weaving and fabric in the area of texts and rituals without addressing problems of iconological interpretation.

Although we concluded that the fundamental gesture of weaving is this interlacing of the warp and the woof of which Plato spoke in *The Statesman*[13]—an interweaving signifying the union of opposites—we were also careful not to apply this conclusion to iconology too hastily. Keeping the images more or less separate, at least temporarily, we first wanted to understand how the interlacing of the warp and the woof—which the Kabyle weaver aptly calls the "soul" *(er-ruh)* of the fabric[14]—renders our metaphor operational in the various fields of application we chose to study.

Two additional and important areas of study, biology and atomism, also contain metaphors of bodily "tissue" and of the "weaving" of the elements of the physical world. Because we considered these disciplines too far outside our areas of expertise, we limited our discussion of them to two appendices.

Finally, the book reflects a purely practical limitation: because we performed our research in common and over several years, the resulting work does not reflect our "individual creativity." On the other hand, this limitation forced us to remain relatively succinct, faithful, as it were, to a certain Navaho custom according to which one should exercise moderation in weaving and which even prescribes cures against excesses of the craft. The same Navaho wisdom also advises weavers not to finish their work completely, but to leave an opening somewhere within it.[15] In our own way, we followed this advice, opting for a relatively concise essay over an erudite tome.

I

PEPLOS

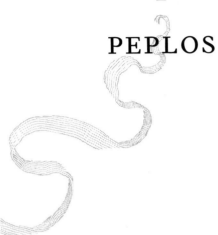

I

FROM THE SIXTEEN WOMEN
TO THE WEAVER KING:
POLITICAL WEAVING
IN GREECE

AMONG the representations the Greeks made of society, of the bonds between men and the cohesion of human groups, or even of the city, there is one that seems to *fabricate* society more than any other: weaving. Domestic or political, profoundly ritualized, weaving brings into play an ensemble of notions capable of being inscribed in the collective memory, gestures that allow one to grasp, to touch, social organization. As much as sacrifice, whose gestures of sharing and distribution define the society in terms of commensality,[1] the practice of weaving—furnishing men and gods with clothing and blankets—offers a simple model to the mind seeking ideas about the nature of social cohesion: how is it that the human group, the family alliance, and the city can hold together? How should they do so? More than the metaphor of the ship of state, the logic of which transfers the problem of internal cohesion "to the outside" (the external menace obliging men to submit to the common good),[2] weaving demonstrates for both the hand and the eye a possible, or desirable, way to conceive of life in society. And it does so in a manner unlike that of sacrifice, in which "to divide is to unite," that is, in which the cutting up and distributing of the animal's body establishes bonds among the participants. Instead, weaving unites what must be united. To weave is to unite, to interlace, to bind: the act is so straightforward that it requires no explanation.

This clear gesture appears in a ritual recorded by Pausanias. After describing the temple of Hera at Olympia in the first of his two books devoted to Elis—the region of the northwest Peloponnesus—the author continues: "Every fourth year there is woven for Hera a robe [*peplos*] by the Sixteen Women, and the same also hold games called Heraea. The games consist of foot-races for maidens . . . These too have the Olympic stadium reserved for their games, but the course of the stadium is shortened for them by about one-sixth of its length. To the winning maidens they give crowns of olive and a portion of the cow sacrificed to Hera. They may also dedicate statues with their names inscribed upon them."[3] Pausanias furnishes two successive explanations for these feminine Olympic Games, which appear to have been more local than the "real" Games. One dates them back to the period when the tyrant of Pisa, a certain Damophon,[4] had just died, after having done a great deal of harm to the Eleans. As the Pisans refused to continue on the path of their lost tyrant and as the Eleans demonstrated their readiness to forget the past, one especially venerable woman was chosen from each of the sixteen cities of Elis to work together to settle their differences. And these sixteen women "made peace" between Pisa and Elis, says Pausanias, who adds: "Later on they were entrusted with the management of the Heraean games, and with the weaving of the robe for Hera."[5] A special house was assigned to them (comparable to the Chitōn in Sparta, where the garment of worship for Apollo was made),[6] located in the agora of Elis,[7] a city about twenty kilometers northwest of Olympia. Of the sixteen cities, *poleis*, which originally sent the women to weave Hera's dress, there remained at the time of Pausanias only eight "tribes," *phulai*, each of which therefore sent two women.[8]

Thus the hostilities between Pisa and Elis were put to rest thanks to the intervention of a first "college" of sixteen aged, noble, and respected women. The chaos of war gave way to peace—a peace so admirably concluded that only the collective weaving of a cloak for the statue of Hera at Olympia seemed adequate to commemorate it. We know that in Artemidorus' interpretation of dreams, "all the auxiliary operations in preparation for the weaving of the cloth signify major concerns, a great tangle of matters, which can be undone only later and with great difficulty," but that "once the fabric has been woven, each matter will fall into its proper place and allow itself to be handled conveniently."[9] The pertinence of this remarkable observation as to the symbolism of wool work, of *talasiourgikē*, is not limited, as we shall see, solely to the interpretation of dreams.

Once in conflict, the sixteen "little cities"[10] or "villages"[11]—which Pausanias calls *poleis*—now find them-

selves reunited into a small federation thanks to the intervention of feminine wisdom.[12] Unlike the famous
synoecism brought about by Theseus in Athens, which
assembled the various "hamlets" (*dēmoi* or *kōmai*) of Attica
into a great city,[13] this unification is the work of women,
and it therefore seems logical that the bonds of the new
federation should be those of a collective weaving, in which
each weaver represents a given city "tribe"; to ensure the
permanence of the federation, the operation is repeated
every four years. Once its manufacture is completed, the
new fabric is carried from the House of the Sixteen Women
in Elis to the temple of Hera at Olympia, in order to
replace the goddess's old cloak. This conveyance must have
been spectacular, as it displayed to all of Elis the work of
the Sixteen Women, into which the peace of the entire
country was woven or rewoven. The original disorder, the
raw wool, is replaced by an organized fabric, in which each
fiber is in place. To weave is really "to give order to a great
tangle of matters" in order to "put each matter in its proper
place." It is to interweave what is different, contrary or
hostile, in order to produce a unified, harmonious textile,
worthy of covering the great goddess of Olympia herself.

This goddess is also one of the great divinities of
marriage, of the legitimate union of husband and wife.[14]
This is certainly the case at Olympia, where she resides in
her temple not far from that of her husband: Zeus in fact
has a statue within Hera's temple[15] and is thus naturally
affected by the offering of the cloak to his wife. Indeed, it
is as the goddess of marriage that Hera appears in another
story regarding the founding of the Heraea. According to
Pausanias, who also gives the "federal" reason for the Elean

festival, the first *aition* of the Heraea (with which it wo'
be natural to associate the weaving of the cloak for H
even though Pausanias does not do so explicitly) consists,
according to the tradition referred to, in Hippodameia's
gesture of thanks when Pelops married her: to organize the
Games in honor of Hera, Hippodameia gathered the Sixteen Women—for the first time, we imagine—to weave the
goddess's cloak.[16]

And this cloak shares with all other fabric properties
liable to explain its conjugal vocation: every *huphasma*
(woven robe) or *huphos* (web) is made of a vertical *stēmōn,*
a stiff thread sometimes called *mitos* (both of these Greek
words, meaning warp, are masculine), and of a horizontal,
supple *krokē,* sometimes called *rhodanē* (these words, meaning "woof," are feminine in Greek).[17] The threads of the
vertical warp were held in position by stones that served as
weights, *laiai,* which Aristotle compares with testicles[18]
(similarly, the Orphics considered that the *mitos* or "warp
thread" represented sperm,[19] while Seneca speaks of the
"coitus" of the warp and the woof).[20] We should therefore
see the crossing of the *stmōn* and *krokē,* their "interlacing"
(sumplokē),[21] as the union of man and woman, this first
sunoikismos (cohabitation), of which the political *sunoikismos* seems to be the extension or multiplication.[22]

For Hippodameia, who is pleased with her union to
Pelops, the peplos offered to Hera *is equivalent* in some
sense to her marriage: the cloak offered to the goddess of
marriage is the symbolic equivalent of the young bride's
sense of good fortune.[23] Next to the Games, sacrifices, and
choruses (one of which is danced under the name of
Hippodameia),[24] the offering of the cloak woven by the

Sixteen Women thus recalls not only the pacification of Elis but also this union of opposites, of the dissimilar, that marriage represents. Covered in a matrimonial cloak commemorating a royal wedding, Hera enables the spectator to visualize concretely what holds together marriage, whether royal or divine, and the city, in opposing but marvelously ordered threads.

While Hippodameia was the first to have the cloak woven for Hera, one of the first kings of Elis, Endymion,[25] maintains an equally privileged relationship to the goddess of Olympia. According to one tradition he falls in love with her, prompting Zeus quickly to drive him from high in the sky to Hades.[26] But the same Endymion also turns out to be an important character in the early history of the Olympic Games, well before their famous inauguration in 776 B.C. When the Games were resumed after the Flood, in the generation following Deucalion, Endymion was among the organizers: his own sons raced for the succession of the kingdom.[27] In fact this cofounder of the Olympic Games is reminiscent in more than one way of Hippodameia, the initiator of the Heraea and of the weaving of Hera's cloak. His name, clearly related to garments, proclaims this loud and clear: apparently derived from *enduein*, "to dress," and, more directly, from *enduma*, "clothing," it actually signifies "the one of the garment." Indeed, it is the basis of mythical stories in which the hero is the victim of an excessive love and of an equally excessive sleep.[28] Why? Because the garment, a large piece of rectangular cloth, also serves as a bed cover. By virtue of his name, the hero seems destined to love as well as to sleep. Is it by chance then that the statue of Endymion at Olympia was wearing

THE CRAFT OF ZEUS

a garment that Pausanias felt worthy of special mention?[29] In any case, the cofounder of the Olympic Games had his tomb at Olympia not far from the place where the bones of Hippodameia were kept.[30] Thus the king of Elis lay practically alongside the queen of Pisa.

Woven to commemorate the peace concluded by the Sixteen Women of Elis, Hera's peplos is reminiscent of another cloak, one more famous than that of the statue of Endymion, namely the *chlaina* imagined by Lysistrata in Aristophanes' comedy, performed in early 411 B.C. during the height of the Peloponnesian war.[31] It is now scarcely two years after the catastrophe of the Sicilian expedition and shortly before the reversal of democracy by the Four Hundred. Lysistrata proposes a political, even federal plan to the city commissioner *(proboulos)*, a plan to correct the muddled affairs of the Athenian empire. This plan is articulated in terms of weaving. "How then would you be capable of appeasing so much disorder and of putting an end to it?" the commissioner asks the women. And Lysistrata responds: "As we do with our thread: when it is tangled, we take it and raise it with our spindles here and there. In the same way we would dissolve this war, if we have our way, untangling the thread by means of ambassadors sent here and there."[32] The affairs of the city thus resemble a ball of wool whose threads are tangled; one untangles them with a spindle, just as one untangles the war thanks to the ambassadors of peace. The stage of weaving envisaged here is the one immediately preceding the weaving proper: the ball contains the thread that, when placed on the shuttle, will become the cloth.

Moving in reverse, Lysistrata then develops her metaphor: "First, as one does with raw wool washed in a bath, after removing the sheep dung, on a bed you have to poke out the bad ones from the city and take out the prickles."[33] Thus the city must undergo a cleansing, the first operation in working the raw wool, which eliminates any debris and thorns. No doubt Lysistrata has in mind here the more or less secret groups that are preparing to overthrow the democracy. "Those who have been joined together," she continues, "and made themselves into a solid mass must be separated into their constituent parts and their heads taken off."[34] The second operation in working with wool, the carding, aims here to eliminate political parties and dema-gogues, who function within the democratic system but have their own interests at heart—interests that must be replaced by other, more appropriate ones: "Then one must unite in a basket the common goodwill, mixing both the resident aliens and those who are our friends abroad, and the debtors to the treasury—mix them in as well." Thus, having placed the good elements of the city in the carder's basket, Lysistrata proposes mixing both metics and friends abroad, namely those who remained allies of Athens during the war. And out of concern for Athens' strained finances, she mixes in the "debtors to the treasury," without whom the debts cannot be paid.[35]

"And, by Zeus," she goes on to say, "as for cities that are colonies of ours, we must acknowledge that they are for us like threads of wool fallen down, each one on its own."[36] Among the allies of Athens, who were expected to pay their tribute to her, Lysistrata thus tries, through a re-cuperative gesture, to include the colonies, or "cleruchies," of Athens, considered as "wool fallen down." And all this wool, washed, carded, and gathered in a basket, is now ready to be spun, according to the image that opens the "recovery plan" imagined by Lysistrata. It is undoubtedly in the interest of avoiding repetition that she skips this spinning stage in her conclusion: "Then, taking everyone's wool, bring it, unite it into a single mass, into a fat ball [*tolupēn*], and with this then weave a cloak for the people [*tōi dēmōi chlainan huphenai*]."[37]

As in Elis, here the weaving of the political or federal garment symbolizes the end of a complicated period marked by hostilities and war.[38] Though by necessarily different means, in both cases weaving produces peace—it is the operation thanks to which the city or federation of cities will master its contradictions and assert its unity. The cloak woven for Hera and the *chlaina* woven for the people of the Athenian empire thus symbolize political reconciliation after a period of war.

From this point of view, the remarkable peplos offered Athena by the Trojan women in the *Iliad* seems different, though occurring within a context of war: when the Trojans, in book 6, feel threatened by the success of the Greeks, notably by that of the furious Diomedes, Hector asks his mother to fetch her most beautiful peplos as an offering to the goddess Athena. Carrying in her hands a peplos "that shone like a star," she goes to the temple with the Trojans, where the priestess lays the offering on the knees of the goddess.[39] This ritual is accompanied by a prayer that seems to clarify the meaning attributed to the garment: the women pray to Athena and promise her twelve heifers if she will defend the city against the aggressors[40]—a prayer that will not be granted (as the text itself emphasizes), perhaps for the simple reason that the peplos offered the deity of the city is the work not of Trojans but of Sidonian women: indeed, Homer informs us that the peplos was brought from Sidon by Paris when he brought Helen back to Troy.[41] This is fundamentally different from the situation in Elis or Athens, where the "political" garment is most decidedly indigenous.

In Athens, then, in the mind of the theatrical spectator, the *chlaina* woven for the people is hardly evocative either of the peplos offered to Athena by the Trojan women or of the peplos woven for the statue of Hera at Olympia. Rather, the weaving proposed by Lysistrata is likely to evoke the great cloak offered every four years to Athena Polias, watching over her city from atop the Acropolis. What do we know about this?

Once every four years, at the moment when the cranes give the signal to the Greek peasant to begin his labors (namely in mid-November),[42] two young Athenian girls called *arrephoroi* begin weaving the peplos destined to cover the statue of Athena nine months later, on the occasion of the goddess's birthday.[43] The start of this work is in fact an important element in the festival of the Chalkeia, celebrating Athena Erganē (and Hephaestus) on the last day of the month of Pyanopsion (October–November); and the women who assist the young *arrephoroi* are called *Ergastinai,* "Work Managers."[44] The task of these female weavers, taking over for two males, Akeseus and Helikon (thought to have woven the goddess's first—magnificent—cloak),[45] is to weave the peplos for the ancient statue of Athena Polias, which is reputed to have fallen from the sky and was kept in the Erechtheum at the Acropolis.[46] A gigantomachy, a struggle between gods and giants, is woven into the peplos[47]—in particular, one might imagine, the struggle between Athena and the giant Asterius, whose death is sometimes considered to be the *aition* of the (Small) Panathenaea.[48]

The investiture of the statue of Athena Polias took place at the Great Panathenaea, a festival whose unifying nature is suggested by its very name[49] and which, according to one tradition, was founded by Theseus to celebrate the unification of the "hamlets" of Attica[50]—into a single political "fabric." Every four years on the twenty-eighth of the month of Hekatombaion (July–August), the peplos of Athena was carried in a spectacular procession from the Kerameikos to the Acropolis, where the garment was entrusted to a priest, probably the King-Archon,[51] whose task was probably to "dress" *(amphihennunai)* the statue with the new peplos.[52] This investiture of Athena Polias was the central act of the festival, which included a highly communal sacrifice: the city, its colonies, and allies were all required to furnish cows as victims.[53] Along with the ritual weaving to produce clothes for the city goddess, or even "for the people," the sacrificial sharing aimed to enact and rekindle the social and political unity.[54]

But the procession that brought the peplos to the Acropolis of Athens bore another significant element, for weaving and sacrificial sharing do not exhaust the repertoire of metaphors for the city. Ever since the archaic period, the city had also been considered a "ship," whose crew was its citizens.[55] It was thus an ancient image, and one that was singularly pertinent for colonial expeditions, on which the ship was already the city—before this city made its influence felt on the soil of a distant land.[56] Now, if the analogy was especially valid for the colony-city, it also pertained to the mother-city, particularly if, as in the case of Athens, this city devoted itself to navigation and naval construction: in the course of the fifth century, Athens was practically becoming a city of oarsmen.[57] The goddess of the Acropolis played a role in this: she was the patroness not only of the loom, called *histos* in Greek, and of the plough (part of which is called *histoboeus*),[58] but also, in her own way, of the ship,[59] whose mast is called the *histos* and the sails *histia*. And this is no doubt one of the reasons why Athena's peplos was transported from Kerameikos to the Acropolis raised on a mast in the form of a T, atop a chariot in the form of a ship.[60]

While the "peplophoric" ship was a relatively recent element, though perfectly in place within the tradition of the Panathenaea, one might imagine that the peplos was transported in a less extraordinary fashion during the archaic period. Did the women weavers carry it to the Acropolis themselves? We do not know, but if this were the case, their *peplophoria* would have been reminiscent not only of the figurative documents from the archaic period,[61] but also of Alcman's *Partheneion*—if, in our interpretation of the poem, we take the word *pharos* in the sense not of "plough" but of "cloak," as a fair number of interpreters have done.[62] It is impossible here to enter into a detailed discussion of the passage in question,[63] a passage that we translate as follows: "When, through the divine night, we carry to the Lady of the Dawn the Cloak—like the star Sirius[64]—the Pleiades rise up and fight against us."[65] Alcman's comparison of the *pharos* to a brilliant star here is not an innovation but, as we have seen, a perfectly traditional image: for Homer, a peplos can "shine like a star,"[66] a formulaic comparison that undoubtedly fixes the horizon of expectation of those listening to Alcman's poem. Now, the chorus of young girls carries this shining *pharos* to offer it to the Lady of the Dawn (a divinity who has yet to be identified). Their procession is accompanied by song. In other words, fabric *(huphos)* and hymn *(humnos)* go hand in hand: is the poet Bacchylides not using what seems to be an etymological figure when he employs the metaphor *humnon huphainein*, "to weave a hymn"?[67] We will return to this theme at greater length.

For the moment let us return to Athens. Taking the principal elements of the festival into account, we have reason to consider the Panathenaea as the enactment of three major representations of the city—as a fabric, as a cow (shared at the sacrifice), and as a ship. (The olive tree, whose oil plays an important role in the festival, can be added as a fourth "representation," a term we would replace with "myth").[68] Among these three representations, the first, namely fabric or weaving, occupies a privileged position when Plato, the Athenian, seeks a paradigm for the art of politics. Indeed, an entire dialogue, Plato's *Statesman*, deals with this paradigm (the sacrificial sharing and the ship of state play only minor roles).[69] But while the use of the metaphor of weaving in Plato reminds us of the ritual weaving of Athena's peplos, it is mainly reminiscent of the image developed by Lysistrata in Aristophanes. Indeed, just as one might accuse the Plato of *The Republic* of plagiarism if one were to compare his sketch of the Academy to the Think-Tank in Aristophanes' *Clouds*, so some have thought that the metaphor of weaving in *The Statesman* is borrowed from the comic poet's *Lysistrata*.[70] This is no doubt to misunderstand the way in which political thought was perpetuated in ancient Greece.

Consider, for example, the myth of the Ship of State, which we know from the poems of Alcaeus and Theognis[71] and which we find, at more than two centuries' distance, in the dialogues of Plato, notably in *The Republic*.[72] The exegesis of this myth remained just about the same from the archaic to the classical period; the situation is analogous for the myth of weaving. We are dealing with a common heritage from which Aristophanes and Plato, on various occasions, borrowed ideas, analogies and metaphors, in short *myths*—leaving us with the impression that the comic poet invented some of the major ideas of Platonic philosophy. But as we have already seen, the metaphor of weaving had a place as a political or civic metaphor in rituals that far predate both Aristophanes and Plato.

Since it is through the exegesis of weaving that we have access to the intimate logic of its "myth," we will now move on to a relatively detailed study of Plato's *Statesman*. This should bring to light what the exegesis of weaving in this dialogue has in common with the rituals of Elis and of Athens and, no less importantly, what specifically philosophical dimension it may carry. What happens to the myth of weaving when it is expressed in a philosophical context?

After dismissing the figure of the "Shepherd King" as belonging to an irrevocable past, a few pages before the middle of *The Statesman*, Plato finally brings into play the paradigm of weaving: "Well then, what example is there on a really small scale which we can take and set beside kingship, and which, because it comprises an activity common to it and to kingship can be of real help to us in finding what we are looking for?" the Stranger asks the young Socrates. "By Zeus,[73] Socrates, I believe I know one. Do you agree that, if there is no other example ready to hand, it would be quite in order for us to select the art of weaving for the purpose [*tēn huphantikēn (technēn)*]?"[74] This selection of a manual activity as a paradigm—and one that is normally feminine to boot (even though King Arkas invented it and, as we recall, Akeseus and Helikon wove the first peplos for Athena Polias)[75]—is problematic for Plato, as we learn further along: "I cannot think that any reasonable person would want to search for a definition of the art of weaving just for its own sake." To study weaving for the sake of weaving would essentially be to lower oneself to a level unworthy of a free man. "But," adds the Stranger, "there is a paradox here which, it seems to me, most thinkers have failed to notice. Likenesses which the senses can grasp are available in nature to those real existents which are in themselves easy to understand, so that when someone asks for an account of these existents one has no trouble at all—one can simply indicate the sensible likeness and dispense with any account in words."[76] Thus while in need of the paradigm of weaving, without which it would be impossible, at a preliminary stage, to account for politics, Plato immediately takes his distance with respect to this paradigm, a two-pronged move that could be characterized as typically Platonic: recall, for instance, that in *Timaeus* the metaphor of the Artisan allows the philosopher to formulate an entire cosmology, despite his disdain for artisanal activity.[77] Similarly, the metaphor of writing, namely "writing in the soul," is based on a profound disdain for writing in its usual sense: while belittling the latter, Plato as it were ennobles its figurative form.[78] Thus weaving is also belittled, which is all the more remarkable as Plato proves to be obsessed both by writing and by weaving in the usual sense of the words.

In fact it is by employing an analogy taken from the learning of letters, *grammata*, that Plato introduces the paradigm of weaving. Writing, which creates "interlacing" *(sumplokai)*,[79] is in effect the "paradigm of the paradigm"[80] here, allowing Plato to define the role he will give to weaving in his inquiry into politics: just as the one who is learning to read goes from easy syllables, which serve as paradigms, to more difficult syllables, ultimately becoming capable of identifying the latter thanks to comparisons with the former, so the dialectician practices on easy paradigms in order to become capable of later deciphering the more complex "syllables of reality."[81] And the easy paradigm, for the definition of statesmanship, is weaving.[82] But it must be emphasized that for Plato, neither this "easy" paradigm nor the definition of politics it will produce is the goal of the discussion between the Stranger and the young Socrates. Just as spelling questions do not aim to teach the spelling of the particular word (although this is a necessary step) but to develop general competence, so the study of weaving as a paradigm for politics targets neither the particular example, as we have seen, nor the thing that it enables us better to define: "How then does this principle apply to our present search for the statesman? Why did we set ourselves the problem? Is our chief purpose to find the statesman, or have we the larger aim of becoming better philosophers, more able to tackle all questions?—Here too [as in the case of learning to spell], the answer is clear; we aim to be able to solve all problems."[83]

Having defined the general paradigm thanks to the paradigm of writing, Plato proceeds to the technical definition of his particular example, weaving. To aid in the definition of statesmanship, the place and properties of the *huphantikē technē* must be specified. Among artisanal activities taken as a whole, the art of weaving produces a product that aims to "protect against suffering," to serve as a "defense," but to do so peacefully, as a "screen": indeed, it is a kind of "housing" consisting not of a roof but of a "cloth" *(skepasma)*.[84] This close relationship between roof (or housing) and cloth is not solely the product of the taxonomic operation but a relationship that we will encounter on several occasions later on. And from "cloth," a term that is still too general, we ultimately arrive at the cloth made of assembled pieces, the garment, which is practically identical with the fabric.[85]

Thus separated from its "origins," weaving must next be distinguished from the "arts exercising a closely similar function to it."[86] For there is work with the wool that precedes weaving itself, beginning with carding: despite what Aristophanes says in *The Birds*,[87] "carding" is not synonymous with "weaving," and the "carder" is not a "weaver."[88] Similarly, spinning, producing warp and woof, cannot be confused with weaving. Along with fulling and darning, these are the arts that "dispute with the weavers' mastery. They are ready to concede to weaving a very considerable part of the whole province of clothesworking, but at the same time they demand the assignment of no small part of it to themselves."[89] *Talasiourgikē*, "woolwork-ing," includes all these arts, which are divided in two according to whether they separate or combine: carding separates, spinning combines; and, significantly, weaving does both, given that the shuttle first *separates* warp and woof[90] and later *combines* them into a fabric. It separates the better to combine. The Stranger concludes this meticulous analysis as follows: "When the section of the art of combination which is also a section of the art of woolworking produces a fabric by the due intertwining of warp and woof, we call the finished fabric a woolen garment and the art superintending its production the art of weaving."[91]

After a long digression into "due measure," the interest of which appears only later in the dialogue, the Stranger returns to "statesmanship, our real subject, and set[s] beside him for comparison the art of weaving as we have just defined it."[92] Already separated from his kin in the pastoral domain, namely shepherds, the king will now figure, like the weaver, within the framework of arts that are either contributory or rivals. Thus, "every art which fashions any object, large or small, which ministers to the needs of an organized human community, must be classed as 'contributory'":[93] instruments, containers, carriages, defenses, diversion, raw or basic material, nourishment—these are the products of the contributory arts in the city. But just as, for example, carders and spinners "disput[e] the fashioning of clothes with the weavers," there are those in the city "who really dispute the fashioning of the web of state with the king,"[94] that is, the exercise of the royal function. Among them, the slaves, as one would well imagine, are quickly disqualified, as they "cannot possibly claim any share in the practice of the art of ruling."[95] Next come the merchants, who play a connecting role among the contributory arts: placing themselves of their own volition at the disposal of others, they cannot dispute the province of the ruler either.[96] As for the specialists in oral and written communication, heralds and clerks, they too are "servants" and not rulers.[97] As for the soothsayers and priests—and among the latter the Stranger mentions in particular the King-Archon in Athens (undoubtedly responsible for covering Athena with her "political cloak")[98]—they are only servants, despite their great social standing.[99] In fact the only rival who is really a menace to the king are the sophists, who are "hard to distinguish from real statesmen and kings; yet we must distinguish them and thrust them aside if we are to see clearly the king we are seeking."[100]

It is only after an elaborate evaluation of political constitutions (monarchy/tyranny, aristocracy/oligarchy, democracy with obedience to laws/democracy in contravention of its laws, and the "seventh,"[101] which is "like a god among mortals")[102] that we return to the rivals of the real king. The sophists and all the "leaders of bogus governments . . . themselves as bogus as their systems . . . supreme imitators and tricksters" who inhabit six of the seven defined constitutions, are forbidden to exercise the royal function.[103] But there remains another group of auxiliaries, who are to politics, for instance, what carders are to weavers: this one includes the rhetoricians, generals, and judges. None of them reaches the level of royal science, to which, on the contrary, they are all servants.[104]

Thus, after these long elaborations on the analogy between weaving and politics, between *huphantikē* and *poli-*

tikē, the Stranger is in a position to conclude that the art that, in the city, "weaves all into its unified fabric with perfect skill" is statesmanship.[105] Until this point the analogy between weaving and statesmanship has been explored solely in view of their *places* relative to their respective auxiliaries and rivals. Now the target changes: the analogy will be developed on a technical level, on the level of the interweaving of threads, which will bring to light the exact composition of true political knowledge. The "due measure" digression has already prepared the way.

"Now that all the classes of arts active in the government of the state have been distinguished, shall we go on to scrutinize statesmanship and base our scrutiny of it on the art of weaving which provides our example for it?" asks the Stranger, introducing this last and fundamental stage in the demonstration.[106] And he proposes to expose the nature of the kingly *sumplokē*, how it is done and what kind of fabric is obtained. Opposing "courage" and "moderation," *andreia* and *sōphrosunē*, he points out that courage, though opposed to moderation, is as much a part of goodness as the latter.[107] Contrary to what is generally asserted, the parts of goodness are thus not always friends: *andreia* and *sōphrosunē* are in reality enemies. The nature of their relationship is defined by the word *stasis*, "civil strife."[108] It is with the word *andreia*, says the Stranger, that we praise actions marked by vigor; conversely, it is with the word *sōphrosunē* (or its synonym *kosmiotēs*) that we laud actions characterized by slowness or gentleness. On the condition, of course, that these actions are not unfitting: for, in that case, we condemn them for exceeding due measure by being either too violent or too indolent. Those whose actions are characterized in this way are inevitably perceived as enemies, praising their own *andreia* and *sōphrosunē* and criticizing the ways of those who are opposed to them, foreigners, enemies. Their relations are marked by enmity *(echthra)*.[109]

When one of these "parts of goodness" comes to dominate an entire city, it becomes an illness, "the most inimical of all the plagues which can threaten the life of a community."[110] For left to themselves, the *sōphrones* stagnate in such tranquility that they end up sliding from freedom into slavery. The *andreioi*, impelled by an excessive passion for war, lead their city to ruin.[111] Excessive gentleness or excessive violence: in either case, the fact of isolating the *sōphrosunē* or the *andreia* turns out to be destructive. How, in effect, can one impose "due measure" on both?

After a "test by games," politics entrusts subjects to educators while retaining "direction and oversight of them all the time . . . [as] the *huphantikē* hands over the materials it intends to use for the fabric to the carders."[112] The individuals who can be taught neither *andreia* nor *sōphrosunē* will be eliminated (for example, by the death penalty); for some, marked by their ignorance and groveling subservience, slavery will be the solution.[113] For those who remain, some will naturally tend toward *andreia:* they will have their place in the warp, the more firm, virile part of the cloth (*stēmōn*, masculine); others, more inclined toward *sōphrosunē*, will constitute the supple and feminine part of the same cloth (*krokē*, "woof," feminine).[114] But before crossing the *stēmōn* and the *krokē* in marriage, where, as we shall soon see, the "stiff" *andreia* and the soft *sōphrosunē* have nothing to do with the real, biological, sex of the individuals concerned, Plato proposes "uniting" the parts of goodness—courage and moderation—through education, a preliminary step that will be the condition for the fabric by marriage.[115]

In the education that politics should provide, explains the Stranger, the immortal part of the soul must in effect be "linked" to the element of goodness it is lacking: thus the *andreia* will be tempered by a divine notion of justice, which politics will arouse in the courageous individual.[116] This "divine link" between courage and moderation, a link that is established, through education, in the individual's soul, is in contrast to the network of links *(desmoi)* created by marriage,[117] and it is to these links that Plato devotes the rest of his dialogue.

In matrimonial alliances, says the Stranger, one makes the mistake of "hailing with delight those who are like themselves and of disliking those who are different."[118] Thus moderate natures look for moderate partners, and "so far as they can, they choose their wives from women of this quiet type" and subsequently marry their daughters into it; the *andreioi* behave in the same fashion. Thus, in the space of a few generations the latter will degenerate into sheer fury and madness, while the others, out of the same refusal to mix, will end up in a state of equally total infirmity.[119] And here is where our kingly weaver comes in. Having given rise to "a conviction about values and standards shared by both types of character"[120] through education, he has prepared his political work, which is "never to allow the gentle characters to be separated from the brave ones; to avoid this he must make the fabric close and firm by working common convictions in the hearts of each type of citizen and making public honors and triumphs serve this end, and finally, each must be involved with the other in the solemn pledges of matrimony. When he has woven his web smooth and 'close-woven,' as the phrase goes, out of men of these differing types, he must entrust the various offices of state to them to be shared in all cases between them."[121] In such a city, one may hope to find a leader who combines the two "parts of goodness"; where governing is done by several, attention must be paid that the equilibrium between *andreioi* (necessary for action) and *sōphrones* (necessary for reflection) be respected.

Thus the weaver king creates "the finest and best of all fabrics,"[122] a fabric "for the people," as Lysistrata had already said, a fabric in which the opposing forces of the city are mastered for the benefit of social peace—a concept that the Sixteen Women of Elis understood well before Plato. Indeed, we are led to consider the metaphor of weaving developed by Plato in *The Statesman* not as a metaphor invented ad hoc by the philosopher, but as the philosophical exegesis of ritual weaving such as it was practiced in Elis by the Sixteen Women or in Athens by the *arrephoroi* and the *ergastinai* or by others still in Sparta (weaving of Apollo's *chitōn*) or in Argos (the festival of the *Endumatia*, which was in all likelihood devoted to the "investiture" of Hera).[123] This philosophical exegesis no doubt has the same essential elements as other exegeses of the same "myth" that must have circulated but of which we have little trace: for example, the insistence with which Plato speaks of the enmity between *andreia* and *sōphrosunē* may have surprised the philosophic commentator of the dialogue but can undoubtedly be explained as a fundamental feature of the common—"popular"—exegesis of the *stēmōn* and the *krokē*, of the interlacing of the masculine warp and the feminine woof in conjugal love.

We should also mention a linguistic fact that was likely to underlie the idea of political weaving for all Greek speakers: the word *stasis*, "civil strife," qualifying the relationship between *andreia* and *sōphrosunē*, is derived from the same verb as *histos*, "loom, cloth," from *histanai*, "to stand something up." Indeed, for Plato, the social or political fabric is but a skillfully mastered civil war. This is an idea that the philosopher undoubtedly borrowed from tradition, in which politics is sometimes a war without arms: let us recall the end of the *Odyssey*, for example, in which the adversaries' arms "dropped from their hands" *(epi chthoni pipte)* so that the city could be established.[124] On the contrary, the passage on the "divine link,"[125] whose relationship to weaving is less obvious, seems a specifically philosophical and, in truth, rather artificial development, which a less constructed analysis could have easily done without. In our opinion, the philosophical bent of the metaphor of weaving in Plato is thus rather limited: it can be seen in its systematic elaboration rather than in any particular detail of the exegesis.

In any case, what characterizes weaving in Elis, in *Lysistrata*, and in *The Statesman* is its pacifying nature: it masters the opposing forces of the city before they destroy everything. It transforms "conflict"[126] into "marriage,"[127] contradiction into cohesion. Rituals can represent this social peace as well as the comic poet or the philosopher, using the same elementary myth of dissimilar and opposing threads. And the juxtaposition of the athletic competition and weaving, at the Heraea as well as at the Panathenaea, does not contradict this interpretation of the myth. Quite the contrary. As much as the athletic competition, which is capable of transforming "savage" rivalry into knowingly orchestrated competition and which brings out what is best in the community as a whole, political weaving uses its own contradictions to its advantage, which is to say to the advantage of the city. This phenomenon, indeed, leads us to think that rituals, repeated every four years at the civic festivals in Elis and Athens and daily in domestic weaving, long nourished political reflection by offering elements capable of structuring a certain idea of the city—with "woolworking" as a great metaphor for an entire process of classification and organization, of hierarchy and government, of interlacing and social bonds, a metaphor already eloquently employed by Aristophanes and pushed to its extreme by Plato.

There is one last point upon which the ritual weaving of the Sixteen Women and that of the weaver king in Plato converge in a very significant manner: the two-pronged exegesis of the ritual of the Sixteen Women, which explains the origin of the weaving of Hera's peplos in terms of both political peace and matrimonial union, corresponds to the strategic place occupied, in the *politics* of the weaver king, by the institution of *marriage*. Matrimonial union and the cohabitation of spouses appear, in effect, to be the elements that form the city, which is also perceived as a "cohabitation" on a large scale. It is thus appropriate to emphasize once again that the word *sumplokē* designates both the physical union of the spouses and the interlacing—whether metaphorical or otherwise—of the threads of the fabric, and to recall that the word *sunoikismos* designates not only the "cohabitation" of spouses under a single and same roof but also, after the unification of Attica by Theseus, the "cohabitation" of Athenians in a city woven, in one piece, "for the people."

Once the peace has been concluded thanks to the Sixteen Women, the "cohabitation" of the Eleans also becomes two-pronged. And if the king of Elis is not a "weaver king" (a title that is more suited to his Arcadian neighbor, King Arkas, the inventor of weaving),[128] he is no doubt a "garment" king, as we have already recalled: Endymion, "the one of the garment," ruled the city where the Sixteen Women wove the peplos—for the goddess loved *by the same Endymion*.[129] The ritual of weaving in Elis is thus inscribed at the heart of Elean mythology. It is not, as has been thought, a simple importation or adaptation of a foreign usage, namely the weaving of Athena's peplos in Athens.[130] Behind Pausanias' two-pronged exegesis of the Elean fabric lies the figure of the royal garment, worn by the king in love with Hera and already symbolizing the unity of the kingdom. In Elea, with Elis and Pisa-Olympia as two opposing poles,[131] this unity could occur only by means of a *sumplokē*. And it is no doubt this polarity of the region that is responsible for the remarkable insistence with which Elea turns itself into a fabric, a royal or divine garment, transforming its own contradictions into solid bonds.

2

"INVESTITURE," *PEPLOPHORIA,*
LUSUS TROIAE: POLITICAL
WEAVING IN ROME

AT A PARTICULARLY dark moment of the Gracchi era,
in the year 125 B.C., disturbing omens began occurring in
Italy: wheat grew on trees; at Veii, it rained oil and milk;
at Arpi, stones; and for the first time in eight years, the owl
was heard on the Capitol.[1] Included in this series of omens
was the birth of an androgyne reported by Phlegon of
Tralles: "In Rome, an androgyne was also born . . . For
this reason, the Senate asked the decemvirs to consult
[*anagnonai*] the Sibyl's oracle. The decemvirs performed an
exegesis [*exhēgēsanto*] of the oracles, the content of which
was as follows: 'The fate of mortals, who discover their
individual paths only after the fact, what omens and what
sufferings divine Destiny prepares for them, will be revealed by my *histos* ["loom" or "fabric"].'"[2] In fact Phlegon
cites two seemingly distinct oracles that prescribe rituals
thanks to which the danger foretold by the birth of the

androgyne will be averted. The first, the beginning of which we have just read, advises the offering of a treasure of silver to Demeter and the sacrifice of oxen to Zeus, of white cows to Hera *(Juno Regina)*, and of drink offerings, notably to Persephone.[3] The second oracle prescribes the offering of richly woven garments to Persephone, the sacrifice of a black cow to Hades, the sacrifice of white goats and a prayer to Apollo, the sacrifice of a white cow to Hera, a song sung by virgins of noble birth, the installation of a *xoanon* (wooden image) for Hera, drink offerings to this same goddess, and a sacrifice to the chthonian deities.[4]

Obviously these are rites of considerable importance; among them, the one described at the beginning of the second oracle is of the most direct interest to us (we will return later to the Sibyl's *histos*). The two verses in question translate as follows: "Dress the venerable Persephone in decorated garments [*huphasmata poikila*] in order for the misfortunes to end."[5] Thus, the oracle simultaneously prescribes the ritual and specifies its intention.

In this case, the "misfortunes" of which the oracle speaks are necessarily political in nature;[6] for the same year, in the absence of Gaius Gracchus, the consul Marcus Fulvius Flaccus had proposed that citizenship be granted the Italic allies of Rome, a proposal that did not obtain the necessary support. As a result the Fregellae defected, and the consul left Rome so as not to have to lead against the rebels the punitive expedition which he had, to all appearances, instigated. The other consul crushed the rebellion, and the partisans of Gaius Gracchus were accused of having favored the defection movement. In Rome, the latter's arrival was awaited: eight years earlier, terrible omens had preceded the death of his brother, and the same thing seemed on the verge of happening again now.[7]

Thus at the moment when the omen of the androgynous child and the consultation of the Sibylline books occurred, civil war was threatening Rome with the defection of allies and divisions reaching the highest level of the city itself. Given the prospect of a civil war, the garments offered Persephone therefore take on a propitiatory significance: the offering seems an attempt to tell the goddess not to forsake the city and to show clemency by sparing the lives of its citizens. But if at this very moment the oracle prescribes offering *huphasmata poikila* so that her cult statue will be dressed in them, we might also imagine that the community wishes to manifest the unity and cohesion that should ideally belong to it. The rifts or dissension of the consuls must be countered with accord; the torn garment must be countered with one that is intact, provided, of course, that weaving follows the same logic in Rome as in Greece. This is apparently the case here. For as far as this ritual goes, everything happens *Achaisti*, "in Greek fashion," to employ the oracle's very words.[8] Thus the city weaves its bonds in the fabric, in keeping with the tradition that we have studied in the preceding chapter. This fabric will cover the goddess of Hades, who is the daughter of Demeter as well as the wife of Pluto.

Moreover, if on a symbolic level the birth of the androgynous child seems to block the smooth functioning of reproduction by making sexual differentiation impossible, a fabric whose principle resides both in the *differentiation* between the warp and the woof and in their *subsequent union* is a singularly appropriate response to this disordered state. The androgyne, who unites what should be separate and who is consequently incapable of uniting with others in a normal manner, is in a certain way the opposite of a fabric, whose warp and woof are spun separately. The androgyne is in some sense the premature fusion of the warp and the woof, whereas it is important to the city to keep separate at the outset what is later to be united.[9] The presence of garments destined for Persephone at the very beginning of the second oracle is structurally significant in the context of the event to which these garments respond, as well as with respect to the context of the civil war: if the androgyne makes the union of opposites impossible, given that it already incorporates them, civil war does so as well, given that it *rejects* their union. Yet one has to wonder why the *huphasmata* are offered to Persephone, a chthonian divinity, rather than to Hera (although there are enough significant lacunae in the text to allow for the hypothesis that an "investiture" of Hera, notably of her new cult statue, figured in it as well). Is this a way of saying that the dangers are native rather than foreign, that they emerge from Roman soil, that the rift is indigenous?[10]

In any case, when, barely a century later, the enemy is not internal but from Carthage, it is to Hera, or rather to Juno, that the Roman matrons offer a cloak *(palla)*.[11] The situation seems desperate: it is the worst moment of the Second Punic War, when, "their faces stricken, their eyes filled with tears, the troop of mothers advanced," carrying the garment they have vowed to the goddess.[12] Naturally, Silius Italicus, our only witness to this *peplophoria*, may be suspected of Homerizing in this passage, for he clearly remembers the peplophoria of book 6 of the *Iliad,* in which the Trojan matrons offer a peplos to Athena with the intention of shifting the fortunes of war in their favor.[13] This is undoubtedly why we do not find the ritual described by Silius in the manuals of Roman religion. But given the "investiture" of Persephone that we have just considered, the offering of a cloak to Juno cannot be considered an isolated fact, solely the product of an imagination imbued with Homer; thus to discount a witness as erudite as Silius for the sole reason that the ritual he relates is not attested in the other sources concerning the Second Punic War would be to use poor methodology.

"We offer you this splendid and regal gift made of golden threads," say the matrons, "which our hands wove and embroidered with a needle. Until the mothers' fears are assuaged, during this time, goddess, you will wear this garment [*hoc tibi . . . uelamen erit*]."[14] And, they add (as a vow), if the goddess would like to help the Romans cast off the enemy, she will also wear a golden crown,[15] another symbolic object whose principle resides in its interlacing, in *sumplokē* (we thus have good reason to believe that the Latin poet knew the fundamental significance of weaving and fabric). Unlike the Trojans, the Romans have created the garment offered the goddess with their own hands, which, in our opinion, is a necessary condition for the offering to be effective. And so it will be. Unlike the Trojan Athena, Juno will *wear* the garment that is offered her; it will not remain on her knees[16] but, like the promised crown, will decorate the cult statue. Like Persephone in the Sibyl's oracle, Juno will be wrapped in a cloak that is *poikilos,* resplendent in its rich designs.

Thus we cannot doubt the existence, in Roman territory, of *peplophoria* and (still in the etymological sense of the word) investiture rituals in response to situations of crisis or war, by which the community attempts to retrieve or assert its unity through the symbolism of a garment and the interlacing of the threads in weaving. The editor of the Sibylline oracles, Hermann Diels, takes his commentary even further: if the annalistic tradition does not mention the ritual by which Persephone receives her *huphasmata poikila*, it is because this practice "is so common that it does not need to be mentioned; it is simply considered to go without saying."[17] Without going this far, we are nonetheless of the opinion that the symbolism of the political or *polias* garment is present as much in Rome as in Greece. It is with this conviction that we now approach the study of another ritual, one that at first glance is unrelated to garments: the *lusus Troiae*, the "Trojan Game," known mainly thanks to an important passage in book 5 of Virgil's *Aeneid*.

Celebrated on the occasion of imperial funerals, *ludi saeculares*, the founding of a temple, or a victory, the reputedly ancient *lusus Troiae* seems to have been revived by Caesar, who had it performed upon his triumph in 46 B.C.[18] We are not in a position to specify the date at which it ceased to be celebrated. We do know that a *lusus* was given at the time of Sulla;[19] on the other hand, it is impossible to know if the participation of young people on foot and on horseback in the *ludi Romani* during the time of the Second Punic War can be interpreted as the celebration of a *lusus Troiae*.[20] But it was under Augustus that the *lusus* took on new importance. Suetonius tells us that the emperor "often used boys of two different ages in the *lusus*

Troiae" because he felt that "to highlight the value of an illustrious lineage in this way was a noble custom from the past."[21] This is no doubt an overly elliptical justification, by which Augustus merely evoked the prestige that this equestrian exercise conferred on the participants and their families. We would therefore be ill-advised to limit ourselves to this explanation (as has been done),[22] as if the goal of restoring the *lusus* were merely to train new warriors by means of a public test. The occasions on which it was celebrated do not seem in keeping with such a practical function.

The future Augustus gave a *lusus* during the *ludi Apollinares* of 40 B.C., as well as in 29 upon his victories and the dedication of the temple of Caesar. He celebrated another in 11 B.C., for the dedication of the theater of Marcellus, as well as on several other occasions *(frequentissime)*. Under Caligula, the *lusus* was performed in 38, during the dedication of the temple of Augustus and during the funeral of Drusilla. Under Claudius, it was given in 47, on the occasion of the festival celebrating the eighth centenary of Rome. Although we have fewer testimonies after this date, there is every reason to believe that the *lusus* continued to be celebrated, since we know that it was performed in 204 during the secular games, as well as in 211 during the funeral of Septimius Severus.

There is no lack of modern interpretations of the *lusus Troiae*. On the basis of the funereal context of some of its celebrations, certain commentators have supposed that the *lusus* was intended to protect either the deceased against aggression or, thanks to a magical sealing of the tomb, the living against an eventual return of the dead.[23] It has also been conjectured that the actors of the *lusus* symbolically led the soul of the deceased toward the underworld.[24] Certainly, ancient sources can be cited in support of each of these interpretations. But the truth is that by neglecting the logic of the *lusus* itself, the interpreters have ignored the only path open to us for its comprehension. Before attempting to define its relationship to the ceremonies with which it is associated, it is necessary to look at the *lusus* head on, in order to outline its principle. From this perspective, even the elliptical explanation given by Augustus is far more pertinent than the avalanche of quotations on the magic of the circle or the descent to the underworld, quotations likely to excite readers with a taste for the esoteric, but which shed little light on the *lusus*.

As we have said, the principal source for the *lusus Troiae* is the description given by Virgil in the *Aeneid*.[25] In this passage, the ritual is celebrated by young Trojans during the first anniversary of the death of Anchises. Before the arrival of the troop of boys, Aeneas himself commands the crowds away from the arena. Under the admiring gaze of their parents, the young men advance on their horses: armed with spearshafts, they form three troops. Each troop includes a troop leader and twelve boys in double file (2 x 6) as well as two armor-bearers. The leaders are Priam (grandson of the king of Troy), Atys (ancestor of the Atii, the family of Augustus' mother), and Iulus (son of Aeneas and Caesar's ancestor). As they parade by, Virgil emphasizes, the Trojans see in them the likeness of their forebears. The *lusus* can begin. The instant the signal is given, the troops separate into two symmetrical and separate "choruses"; upon another signal, they return to their places.

"Next they entered upon other figures too, and reversed these figures, with rank facing rank across a space between; and they rode right and left in intertwining [*impediunt*] circles. And they began a pretence of armed battle, sometimes exposing their backs in flight and sometimes turning their spearpoints for attack. Then they made peace again and rode along in an even line."[26]

This is Virgil's description. Yet the poet adds two images, the first of which seems particularly likely to pinpoint its meaning: the pattern of equestrian movements, he says, is that of the Labyrinth of Minos in Crete. It is true that at first glance this comparison seems to indicate nothing more than the extreme complexity of the movements executed by the young Trojans. But let us read the paragraph more closely: "They say that once upon a time the Labyrinth in mountainous Crete contained a path, woven [*textum . . . iter*] between walls which barred the view, with a treacherous uncertainty in its thousand ways, so that its baffling plan, which none might master and none retrace, would foil the trail of any guiding clues. By just such a course the sons of the Trojans entangle [*impediunt*] their paths, weaving [*texunt*] in play their fleeing and their fighting."[27] In a context that is a far cry from a weaving manual, such a repetition of the verb *texere*, "to weave," and of its synonym *impedire* (expounded upon with *implicare* and *intexere* by Servius, who adds: *a uestibus tractum*, "[metaphor] taken from [the fabrication of] clothing")[28] would seem to be a stylistic error unless the poet wanted to convey that he was aware of the principal figure that underlies the movements of the young warriors: the metaphor of weaving.

The evocation of the Labyrinth is not an obstacle to this

interpretation, for, as we shall see later, the edifice constructed by Daedalus is associated with weaving: it is thanks to the "warp thread" *(mitos)* offered by Ariadne that Theseus, having unraveled it as he advanced, succeeds in finding the exit from the Minotaur's home.[29] As for the second image employed by Virgil to define the movement of young Trojans, "weaving" their fleeing and fighting, it also fits, it seems to us, with the metaphor of weaving: the horsemen are compared to "dolphins that swim through the salt sea-water, cutting the Carpathian or African straits and playing as they cross the waves."[30] Known for their capacity to dance in chorus[31] and to swim in almost military formation, dolphins are linked to their offspring by particularly strong bonds, as we learn in Aelian.[32] But their tight social fabric is made up of individuals in motion: surfacing and diving in their own particular fashion (*emerguntque iterum redeuntque sub aequora rursus*, writes Ovid).[33] the dolphins' movement resembles that of the shuttle, which alternates between passing over and under the threads of the warp in weaving. Although this observation may seem exaggerated, it will seem less shocking in a moment.

For Virgil and his contemporaries, the *lusus Troiae* is first and foremost the "Trojan Game" which the Trojans brought to Italy and which Ascanius (identical to Iulus in Virgil's text), the founder of Alba Longa, would teach the Latins; the Albans in turn taught it to the Romans.[34] Virgil adopts this "historicization" of the term *Troia*, thus rooting the *lusus* in Rome's mythical past. At the same time, he employs a curious expression that—alongside the already-mentioned uses of *texere* and *impedire*—indicates that he also had something else in mind; for in the last verse of the long passage that interests us here, he adds: "And to this day the boys are called 'Troy' and their regiment 'Trojan'—*Troiaque nunc pueri, Troianum dicitur agmen*."[35] This seems to mean that an original "*troia* game" was resemanticized into "Trojan Game." Here we are immersed in "myth."

This "historicizing" resemanticization has been rejected by scholars, who propose an etymology based on a document dating from about 600 B.C. that is often imagined to represent the "Trojan Game." It is a wine pitcher found in Tragliatella, near Cerveteri, bearing the inscription *TRUIA*, which designates a labyrinth (represented on the vase).[36] According to Paul the Deacon, *truare* means *mouere*, "to move, to dance, to play";[37] and according to Suetonius, the *lusus* was generally considered to be a Pyrrhic dance (that is, a war dance).[38] We have therefore interpreted *troia* as a kind of quadrille, or else the place where this dance was performed. It is clear that the sense of "movement," if not of "dance," suits the context, and we have reason to retain this etymology as one of the components of the signification of the *lusus*.[39]

Nonetheless, we must take our investigation further. In the *Glossaria Latina*[40] we read the following definition, which, to our knowledge, has not been invoked in modern research into the "Trojan Game": *troia hē krokē hoc subtemen*. In other words, in Greek *troia* is synonymous with *krokē* (or *rhodanē*), meaning *subtemen* in Latin, "woof" in English. In turn, the lexicographer Hesychius glosses the neighboring word *trōa* with *harpedonē*, "weaving thread."[41] Faced with these perfectly coherent lexicographical facts, we are in a position to think that the Latin *troia* had the same meaning, whether there is a relationship between *troia* and *truare* or not. If we base ourselves on K. W. Weeber's analysis, according to which *TRUIA* is the Etruscan transcription of the Greek word *Troia*,[42] we can suppose that the inscription appearing on the Tragliatella pitcher confers on the representation the sense of "woof."

The same reasoning applies to the game that is central to our inquiry: *lusus Troiae* should be translated as "woof game" or "running thread game," which means that we again find ourselves ensconced in weaving. The *pueri*, one might imagine, constitute the woof of this game, which is regulated in a sense by its own sturdy warp. The references to weaving that we have pointed out in Virgil's text thus take on their true weight: the spectacle presented itself not only as a "weaving" or an "interlacing" for the eye but also, by its very name, as an enactment of the metaphor of weaving.

That said, the boys who participate in the "woof game" are armed.[43] Their cavalcade in effect resembles a kind of simulated tournament that, according to Virgil, includes three clearly defined stages: following a peaceful opening parade, the *pueri* separate and clash, after which peace is restored.[44] What should we make of this *armed aspect*, which was apparent enough[45] for the *lusus* to be commonly called Pyrrhic? Should it be considered in its relation to the defense of Rome, to the season of war, to the ramparts? We do not think so. It is true that the game was celebrated upon the foundation of Alba by Ascanius as well as upon the victories of Caesar and Augustus. We might also, in the extreme, admit that the game defended the city against the dead, against death, when it was executed on the occasion of an imperial passing.[46] But how should we interpret the celebrations organized within the framework of the *ludi Apollinares*, of the *ludi saeculares*, or of the dedication of a monument? Moreover, nothing in the *lusus* itself evokes a foreign war. The combatants who face off are all Romans. The *lusus Troiae* has nothing in common with a ceremony such as the declaration of war next to the *columna bellica:* this column played the role of a territorial border; the fetial (priest) responsible for the declaration took his place near the column and threw a lance into a piece of land purchased by prisoners of war, in other words, by non-Romans.[47] To ritually declare a foreign war, the Romans thus simulated a hostile act, but they all stood on the same side, behind the fetial, and attacked an external enemy.

During the *lusus Troiae*, on the contrary, the simulated aggression is aimed at Romans. Recalling the insistence with which Plato speaks of the "enmity" and of the "civil strife" *(stasis)* between the warp and the woof,[48] we may interpret the hostile phase of the *lusus* as the enactment of the opposition between the parts that constitute all fabric. Without separation, there is no fabric. But there is no fabric either without the union of contraries, without the harmony of opposing elements, without their peace—this peace to which Virgil's text explicitly refers after the description of flight and attack: "Then they made peace again and rode along in an even line."[49] The "woof game" enacts the confrontations that menace the entire community if not held in check. The procession of the *pueri* demonstrates the interplay of forces that must be tempered in order to produce the solid fabric of a city in harmony with itself.

The threat of civil war, of the tearing of the social

fabric, is always lurking at the heart of this harmony. Thus, in celebrating the "woof game," one weaves and reweaves social union, whether in conditions marked by relative political stability or in those of dissension, even of a more or less impending civil war. In times of calm, for instance, the *lusus* is celebrated on the occasion of the foundation of Alba,[50] a celebration that in some sense marks the constitution of the new city. Also in times of calm, it is celebrated on the occasion of the secular games and of imperial deaths.[51] In these instances, one may imagine that the city remakes its entire fabric after a break, whether that of the start of a new "century" or of the disappearance of a prince. Another type of celebration is also suggested by the remarkable vogue of the *lusus* under Augustus.

In 29 B.C., when a *lusus Troiae* was given on the occasion of Augustus' victories and the dedication of the temple of Caesar, it was a time of civil war, provoked by the assassination of the divine Julius. The situation was similar in 40 and in 46, within the framework of Caesar's triumph, as well, perhaps, as when the *lusus* was given at the time of Sulla. Even the one given upon the dedication of the temple of Augustus, in A.D. 37, may be included in this series: it could well symbolize the rejection of internal dissension after the difficult end of a reign.

How might the great Roman families have felt in 46, in 40, or in 29, when the celebration of the *lusus Troiae* was announced? On the one hand, the game unequivocally evoked real, existing confrontations, notably between families from which the *pueri* were recruited. On the other hand, these enemies, new or old, were caught in a bind: Augustus was honoring a reputedly ancient ceremony, declaring that it constituted an excellent occasion for noble families to win renown. Concerned with respect for traditions and with the status of their houses, the aristocrats would have been hard pressed to avoid the celebration, especially if the small number of participants depicted by Virgil corresponded to that of the game performed in the Rome of his day. By authorizing their sons to participate in the *lusus*, the nobles were essentially indicating that the hostilities were over and that they shared, along with the organizer of the game, the same wish for harmony and peace. What is more, the leaders of the three troops were soon the princes of the imperial house, and it seems that the dates on which the *lusus* was celebrated were related to the dynastic calendar: which is to say that the former enemies of Augustus and of the new regime were expressing their agreement with and submission to the Caesars in spectacular fashion. Seen in this light, the warnings of Asinius Pollio—a former republican who weakly rallied to the side of the victor—against the danger of accidents during the *lusus Troiae* were apt to fool no one: what the old republican criticized *grauiter inuidioseque*, "with great bitterness," in the Senate[52] were the clever media traps that the emperor laid for his enemies on a regular basis. By the subtle use of the "woof game"—and subtle it was—Augustus succeeded in turning his adversaries into associates in a social weaving of which he himself was the master weaver.

II

CHLAINA

3

APHRODITE

POIKILOTHRONOS:

EPITHETS, CLOAKS,

AND LOVERS

POSITIONED at the start of the first ode of the first book of Sappho, the epithet *poikilothronos* cannot escape the attention of the poet's readers, especially since it is applied to a divinity of primary importance in her poetry, Aphrodite.[1] From tradition or habit, it is translated as "seated on a richly worked throne." This is how it appears, for example, in the prestigious dictionary by Liddell-Scott-Jones,[2] from which a majority of commentators and translators, right down to David Campbell, have taken their cue.[3] Now, *poikilothronos* is not Homeric: the word, which is impossible to integrate into a hexameter, is notably absent throughout the entire epic. Of course, there is no lack of Homeric passages in which a divinity is seated on a splendid chair; and these passages, as well as a good number of analogous figurative documents, are invoked when the necessity arises to anchor this isolated word—it is in fact unique—in the material reality of the archaic period.[4] Why would such a necessity arise? The classic commentary by Denys Page gives no reason other than the unusual nature of the idea expressed by the epithet, making no mention of the existence of an alternative interpretation, as if it were an issue of unspeakable menace.[5]

As we learn in the etymological dictionaries of Hjalmar Frisk and Pierre Chantraine, the meaning of *poikilothronos* is not as incontestable as one might think upon reading Page's commentary or Campbell's translations. Indeed these two dictionaries favor the meaning "dressed in a cloak with flowered designs."[6] They assign this meaning to Aphrodite's epithet because they consider it to be composed not of *poikilos* and *thronos* ("decorated" and "throne," respectively) but of *poikila* and *throna*. Indeed, these two words appear in a Homeric half-line, in book 22 of the *Iliad*, where the reference is to the cloak Andromache is weaving at the moment when her husband is being killed by Achilles. Homer says in effect that she was "sprinkling brightly colored flowers" into the fabric.[7]

For their interpretation, Frisk and Chantraine rely on an excellent article by Lillian Lawler that appeared in 1948 (and with which we must assume Page was familiar).[8] Using the passage in which Andromache weaves her *throna poikila* as her point of departure, Lawler points out, among other things, that the adjectives that end in -*thronos* are used by Homer only in the feminine, whereas *thronos*, "throne," is almost exclusively a man's chair. An epithet such as *euthronos* cannot be synonymous with *euhedros*, "sitting on a lovely throne," for the simple reason that the latter designates masculine beings as well as feminine.[9] In addition, *thronos* is never qualified as *poikilos* by Homer. But it is primarily the observations of lexicographers that are useful to us here. Quoted in the scholia to Theocritus, Kleitarchos comments as follows: "*throna:* among the Thessalians, the word means 'woven designs'; among the Cypriots, 'flowered clothes' [*anthina himatia*]."[10] Hesychius falls within the same category: "*throna:* the word means 'flowers'; also, 'woven designs of varied colors.'"[11] As we see, this gloss applies perfectly to the passage of the *Iliad* that we have cited. (Note as well that Hesychius explains *throna* as "flowered embroideries.")[12]

For Lawler, Sappho's Aphrodite is thus the goddess "with decorative flowers." Already the elderly Ulrich von Wilamowitz-Moellendorff had envisaged this interpretation, but immediately rejected it. For if the epithet has this meaning, where would the flowers be, he wonders with irritation.[13] Lawler is not unaware of the problem, which she resolves by postulating the ellipsis of a word signifying "cloak" or "robe"[14] (think of the *peplos poikilos*, "decorated cloak," woven and worn by Athena in book 5 of the *Iliad*, described in a passage that provides an important key for the analysis of Sappho's poem).[15] The goddess "with decorative flowers" would thus in reality be a goddess "with a *dress* of decorative flowers." Although the epithet cited by Lawler in support of her hypothesis is poorly chosen,[16] others can be located that are entirely pertinent. In Aristophanes' *Lysistrata*, for instance, Athena is qualified as *chrusolopha*, "with a golden crest," even though, strictly speaking, the epithet is applied to her helmet.[17] But in a certain way this reasoning is futile. For doesn't Kleitarchos specifically say that *throna* can mean "flowered garments"?

This, in fact, is all we need in order to translate *poikilothronos* as "dressed in a cloak with brightly colored flowers," as Lawler, Frisk, Chantraine, and many others have done.[18]

Yet another criticism has been aimed at Lawler. Pointing out that the epithets ending in *-thronos* refer to goddesses and not to their clothing, G. Aurelio Privitera in a 1967 article agrees with Wilamowitz's perspective. But he reasons as follows: even if we accept the meaning proposed by Lawler, this meaning had most certainly been lost in Sappho's time, when the element *-thronos* was understood as referring to a divine or royal throne. In other words, any effort to connect epithets such as *poikilothronos* to *throna* have no practical consequences, since Sappho's contemporaries, not to mention the Greeks of the classical era, would certainly have lost the vestimentary sense of this type of epithet, automatically associating it with the word *thronos*, "throne."[19] For is not Philip of Macedonia *sunthronos* when he "thrones with" the twelve gods in Diodorus Siculus (first century B.C.)?[20]

But let us stop to consider a document from the classical period, one that, quite significantly, brings into play the epithet *chrusothronos*. This is Aristophanes' *Birds*, a play performed in 414 B.C. Upon his arrival in Cloud-Cuckoo-Land, a poet imbued with Pindar begins his brief stay with an invocation to the Muse: "It is Cloud-Cuckoo-Land, the blessed city, that you must celebrate, Muse, in your poetry."[21] Poorly dressed, he naturally hopes to be materially compensated for his odes to the city's glory. Seeing this, Pisthetaerus attempts to get rid of the poet, deciding to give him a fur-lined cloak, a *spolas*. The poet responds:

"My Muse accepts this gift gladly,"[22] but he gives Pis-thetaerus to understand that he also needs a chiton. He receives it instantly and, upon leaving the city, sings: "O Muse *chrusothronos*, you must celebrate the shivering and icy city."[23] Clearly, the epithet refers to the clothing received by the poet and, metaphorically, by the goddess. The Muse, who has no garment epithet at the beginning, receives one by allusion to the fur-lined cloak and the chiton offered in the meantime to her faithful servant. To our minds, this constitutes proof that the garment-related meaning of epithets ending in -*thronos* was still current in Athens almost two centuries after Sappho. By insisting on translating *poikilothronos* as "seated on a decorated throne," we risk incorrectly interpreting one of Aphrodite's essential attributes, namely her "cloak with rich floral designs," which, like an emblem, introduces the work of the great lady of Lesbos.

This cloak is well known to us from other sources. According to Homer, the *peplos ambrosios*, the goddess's "divine robe," was the work of the Graces *(Charites)* themselves.[24] The author of the *Cypria* specifies that the Graces were assisted by the Seasons in their work (in other texts, the *Charites* and the *Horai* are again associated with the goddess's robe): "She robed her body in the garments which the Graces and Seasons had made and dyed with the flowers of spring, even such as the seasons bring—with saffron crocus and larkspur, with the lush violet and the fair blossom of the rose, sweet and nectarous, and with the ambrosial cups of narcissus and lily . . . divine Aphrodite robed herself in garments scented with all the seasons."[25] Although this text presents considerable difficulties, it gives an idea of Aphrodite's clothing, which corresponds perfectly to the definition of *throna* by Kleitarchos: they are truly *anthina himatia*, "floral garments." The abundance of flowers in the fabric described by the poet of the *Cypria* perfectly justifies the first element of the epithet used by Sappho, namely *poikilo-*, which indicates the wealth and variety of the design (and at the same time also subtly classifies Aphrodite as among the divinities with *mētis*, "wisdom, skill, craft").[26] Therefore, when the goddess appears before Anchises in the *Homeric Hymn to Aphrodite*, we are not surprised to find *poikilos* again, or more precisely *pam-poikilos* ("all-bedecked"), among the adjectives qualifying the goddess's *peplos*, that extraordinary garment whose brilliance is greater than the "flame of fire."[27]

Thus, the passage in Aristophanes' *Birds* teaches us that the Greeks of the classical period could associate epithets of the *poikilothronos* type with *throna*, "floral garments" (rather than with *thronos*, "throne"), an association that, from our perspective, seems perfectly motivated by the importance and appearance of the clothing worn by Aphrodite (as for the Muses, they also warrant epithets ending in *-thronos*,[28] as we shall soon see). A passage from book 14 of the *Odyssey* seems to be built on an idea analogous to that encountered in *The Birds*, an idea that may have been in Aristophanes' mind as he was conceiving the poet's brief stay in Cloud-Cuckoo-Land. Let us revisit the passage in question.[29]

Odysseus has just dined with Eumaeus, his faithful swineherd, who has not recognized him. The weather is bad. Odysseus, disguised as a beggar, needs a cloak for the night. Instead of asking the swineherd directly, he makes up a story that will have the anticipated effect. Once, outside Troy, he says, he was lying in ambush with a contingent of Achaeans. Without a cloak *(chlaina)* in the cold night, he asked advice from Odysseus, lying next to him, who solved the problem as follows: under the pretext that reinforcements had to be brought in, but in reality to make a cloak available—in this case a purple one *(chlaina phoinikoessa)*[30]—Odysseus sent a man to the Achaean camp so that his comrade could sleep until dawn. "Wrapped in that man's cloak how gratefully I lay in the bitter dark until Dawn came stitched in gold [*chrusothronos*]!"[31] The attribution of *chrusothronos* to the Dawn here is very likely in reference to the cloak received by the narrator, just as, in Aristophanes, the Muse is qualified by the same epithet once the poet receives the clothing he needs in the cold. Thus even the red color of the cloak seems to play a part: it anticipates in a sense the golden warmth of a *chrusothronos* Dawn.

The vestimentary meaning of the epithet referring to Dawn is confirmed by the first and last lines of book 8 of the *Iliad*. As Cedric Whitman has shown, from a compositional point of view the ensemble of this book is rigorously structured according to an ABC . . . CBA scheme, which is not the result of the book divisions established by the Alexandrian editor.[32] If, at the beginning of this structured ensemble, Dawn is qualified as *krokopeplos*, the meaning of this epithet is clear: Dawn is "saffron-robed." For the Greeks, in fact, no color is closer to gold than saffron, which sometimes functions as its technical substitute:[33] the epithet *krokopeplos* is thus practically synonymous with *chrusothronos* and, one might imagine, evokes not only the color in which the dawn sky is "robed" but also weddings, given that Hymen wears a saffron-colored cloak[34] (recall that Dawn is the *wife* of Tithonos).[35] Now, book 8 ends with another mention of the same goddess: the Trojans spend the night camped in front of Troy while the horses next to their chariots "wait for *euthronos* Dawn." The vestimentary epithet of the first verse corresponds to the vestimentary epithet of the last; for, as we have pointed out, *euthronos* is synonymous not with *euhedros*, "seated on the beautiful throne," but rather with a word such as *euheimōn*, "dressed in beautiful clothing" (just as *poikilothronōs* is synonymous with *poikilheimon*). In other words, if Dawn is *euthronos* or *chrusothronos*, it is not because she "sits on a throne" in the sky but because she is *krokopeplos*.

As a goddess of marriage, Hera is also *chrusothronos*. In a remarkable passage at the end of book 1 of the *Iliad* Zeus settles next to Hera in the marital bed after a day of discord and festivities: "Zeus the Olympian and lord of the lightning went to his own bed, where always he lay when sweet sleep came upon him. Going up to the bed he slept, and *chrusothronos* Hera beside him."[36] We will not disingenuously bemoan the fact that Hera went to bed with her throne: in Homer we know, for example, that the sky can be *asteroeis*, "starry," above warriors who are fighting in the middle of the day.[37] The epithet is not chosen as a function of the situation as it appears but as a function of what the traditional bard *knows* of the sky (Ernst Gombrich studied an analogous phenomenon in the domain of figurative art)[38] or, as Milman Parry would have it, as a function of the economy of formulaic composition.[39] In the passage quoted, Hera's epithet is thus more indicative of the goddess's status than of the presence of a throne in her bed. Yet we have good reason to believe that the goddess's status is expressed by mention not of her throne but of her garment. The importance attributed to Hera's peplos by the Eleans is a first confirmation of this.[40] The *palla* "with golden threads" offered to Juno (= Hera) by the Roman women during the Second Punic War is undoubtedly a second.[41] The wife of Zeus is "wearing a peplos with golden flowers" in her capacity not only as a goddess of the city but also as the goddess of marriage: the two-pronged Elean exegesis for the ritual of the Sixteen Women results from these two aspects of the goddess, the second of which is expressed in the lines cited above from *Iliad* 1. After a day of conflict,[42] husband and wife are temporarily reconciled under a single blanket.

A passage in book 4 of the *Odyssey* presents another married couple lying on the marital bed. We are in Sparta at the time of a wedding (that of Menelaus' natural son). After welcoming Telemachus and his traveling companion, the king and queen are finally going to sleep: "Then deep in the great mansion, in his chamber, Menelaus went to rest, and Helen, queenly in her long gown [*tanupeplos*], lay beside him."[43] As in the scene with Zeus and Hera, we may first note that it is the husband who joins his wife, who is already lying down. Then, in both cases, the wife is qualified by a vestimentary epithet: there is no doubt possible as to the meaning of *tanupeplos*, "with her long peplos." In our opinion, the couple lies together beneath the wife's peplos. In both descriptions, the sequence is structured with respect to this fact: the wife is already in bed, beneath her peplos, when the husband lies down beside her.

The hypothesis that the wife's garment—qualified as *chrusothronos* or *tanupeplos*—and the cover of the marital bed are one and the same seems confirmed by Theocritus' "Epithalamium of Helen." Before the door of the wedding chamber, a chorus of young girls sings, first addressing Menelaus: "Fortunate husband! Someone well disposed took care to assure your success when you came to Sparta like the other princes. You alone of the heroes will have Zeus as father-in-law: it is Zeus's daughter who came under your shared coverlet [*hupo tan mian hiketo chlainan*]."[44] As we may recall, the word translated as "coverlet" in this passage, *chlaina*, also designates a garment: what is being discussed is a large piece of rectangular fabric, woven in wool, which can serve as both a blanket and a cloak (note that in Homer the *chlaina* is always a man's garment).[45] In this instance, the bride lying beneath the *chlaina* is herself a weaver. In the *Iliad* Homer recounts how, deep in her Trojan palace, she wove the battles of the Trojans and the Achaeans into a large cloak;[46] in the *Odyssey* she offered a magnificent peplos, her own handiwork, which "shimmered like a star," as a farewell gift to Telemachus.[47] Theocritus himself in his "Epithalamium" insists a great deal on Helen's excellence as a weaver.[48] Thus it would not be misguided to think that Helen had herself woven the *chlaina* beneath which she lies next to Menelaus.[49] After all, he came to Sparta to become Helen's husband and thus the successor to King Tyndareus. Helen, on the other hand, has always been at home in Sparta. It is thus, in our opinion, not only under her own roof that the couple unites but under her "cloak."

Yet in one specific way the Menelaus-Helen couple is not representative of Greek custom; for normally the wedding ceremony introduces the wife into the home of her future husband. The bride is a foreign element that has to be integrated.[50] Her future spouse receives her beneath his roof and beneath his cloak. In a fragment from Euripides, for example, the young woman is supposed to "end up beneath the *chlaina* of a well-bred husband";[51] here, apparently, the wedding *chlaina* is furnished by the groom and not by the bride. We have already mentioned the peplos Telemachus received from Helen. Penelope would keep it in her home until the day her son gave it to his wife at their wedding: "Keep it for your own bride," says Helen to Telemachus, "your joyful wedding day; let your dear mother guard it in her chamber."[52] The wedding of Kadmos and Harmonia in Thebes follows the same pattern. All the gods came down from the sky to attend; in his own palace, the king offers the peplos to his young bride.[53] Here, the groom is at home, while his wife is foreign. He is the one to furnish the nuptial garment.

But the best example is the story of what one might call the foundation of marriage on Greek soil, told by the pre-Socratic Pherekydes of Syros: "His halls they made for him, many and vast. And when they had accomplished all these, and the furniture and manservants and maidservants and everything else necessary, when everything was ready, they held the wedding. And on the third day of the wedding Zas [= Zeus] makes a great and fair cloth and on

it he decorates Ge and Ogenos and the halls of Ogenos . . .
'for wishing marriages be yours, I honor you with this. Hail
to you, and be my consort.' And this they say was the first
Anacalypteria.[54] from this the custom rose both for gods and
for men. And she replies, receiving from him the
cloth . . ."[55] This fragment is part of the cosmogony of
Pherekydes, who was active during the sixth century B.C.
and whose thought seems to have influenced Pythagoras,
among others.[56] It is true that in his cosmogony the function
of the cloak—also called *peplos*[57]—extends beyond the
nuptial context evoked in the passage cited, for the same
piece of fabric is also placed on "the winged Oak,"[58] a
symbol whose exact meaning escapes us. One might imagine a mast and its sail (the "wings" of a boat being its
sails);[59] it has even been suggested (though probably incorrectly) that the "mast" in question is the one on which
Athena's peplos was mounted during the procession in the
Panathenaea.[60] But these difficulties must not prevent us
from seeing what is perfectly clear in our fragment. For the
text explicitly states that the *pharos* woven by Zas is first
and foremost part of the ceremony from which the wedding
"custom" *(nomos)* is derived. Since that day, this is how
gods and humans have celebrated the *anakaluptēria,* a word
whose literal meaning is "unveiling." The third stage in the
wedding celebration, the unveiling of the bride, is thus the
moment when the groom gives the cloak to the bride in
the wedding chamber. Before this, there is a celebration in
the home of the future bride (first stage), following which
the guests lead the couple to the home of the future groom
(second stage), a migration that goes *oikothen oikade,* "from
one house to the other,"[61] and which, accompanied by the

nuptial song, the Hymenaeus, establishes the link between the respective homes of the betrothed.[62]

The fact that the two first stages of the nuptial ceremony are not mentioned in the fragment by Pherekydes does not necessarily reflect an incomplete transmission of the text. For Zas's bride simply does not have a home from which to come: we have here the very origin of the custom that will later enable the formation of different houses. For this reason, it seems, the text is limited to the rite of *anakaluptē-ria*, on the occasion of which Zas's bride, Chthonie, receives the magnificent nuptial garment with its depictions of Gaia and of Okeanos. We know that, in Pherekydes, Zas curiously transforms himself into Eros in order to be able to create the bonds of harmony and love necessary for the opposing elements of the entire cosmos.[63] This is an interlacing that is essentially weaving. It allows Zas to create not only the wedding cloak but also the union of the bride and groom, beginning with his own union with Chthonie, henceforth elevated to the rank of goddess of marriage (and thus possible to identify with Hera). Both literally and figuratively, Zas is a weaver.[64]

Since, for obvious reasons, Chthonie has no home from which to come, Pherekydes' fragment emphasizes the construction of the palace of Zas. It is here, in his own new home, that the weaver god makes the *pharos* for his wedding. Thus, in this instance, the spouse offers the nuptial garment, which is identical with the shared blanket, to his bride. Now, if this is the custom, some will object, our hypothesis about the *mia chlaina* of Menelaus and Helen is hardly defensible: why assume that Helen furnishes the *chlaina* for the nuptial bed? Her abilities as a weaver are not sufficient reason, for Menelaus undoubtedly could have brought a *chlaina* from Mycenae.

In studying the analysis of the art of weaving in Plato's *Statesman*, we drew attention to the close relationship between "roof" *(stegasma)* and "fabric" *(skepasma)*, between house and cloth, established by the Stranger.[65] We now feel it is appropriate to insist further on this association. We believe in effect that it is up to the spouse already living in the future home of the couple to furnish the blanket beneath which the newlywed's union will be consummated.[66] Most often this means that the offering of the nuptial gift falls to the groom, beginning with Zas. Normally, one seeks one's bride *elsewhere* and introduces her into one's own home. When, exceptionally, it is the man who is integrated into a foreign home, as in the case of Menelaus, he ends up beneath the *chlaina* of his bride without there being any contradiction with respect to the marriage of Zas and Chthonie. Pherekydes' text amply insists on *oikia* and *pharos*, on "house" and "cloak," to make such a hypothesis perfectly credible (especially since these elements are interchangeable in dream interpretation).[67] Indeed, it is as if it fell to the "house" to furnish the cloak. We will now attempt to verify the basis of this close association.

When, early in their travels, the Argonauts arrive in Lemnos, the island is inhabited only by women: the Lemnians had killed their husbands for having been unfaithful.[68] According to Pindar, Queen Hypsipyle invited the visiting heros to compete "for a garment [*esthatos amphis*]" (the same story is told by Simonides, according to the scholiast); "and they united with these women [*kai suneunasthen*]," adds the poet, as if explaining his own statement.[69] Thanks to their promptness, Lemnos is repopulated. Jason himself unites with the queen, who gives birth to a son named Euneos, "the one of the nuptial bed."[70] Apollonius Rhodius, in fact, mentions the garment won by Jason: long after his stay in Lemnos, after bathing in a river, the hero "donned his dark *pharos*, which Hypsipyle of Lemnos had given him once and which recalled their frequent lovemaking [*adinēs mnēmēion eunēs*]."[71] Pollux, another Argonaut, also wore a *pharos* he'd received from a Lemnian.[72] The example of the Argonauts who joined with the Lemnians seems to prove our hypothesis: in Lemnos, the women are at home; for their marriage to the Argonauts, they are the ones to furnish the nuptial *pharos*, and not the men. Women offer the matrimonial cloak if they live in the house where the couple will reside; the man does so if he is the one already living there.

The athletic prelude to the Lemnian marriages evokes another passage in Pindar, from the ninth *Pythian*. After assassinating their bridegrooms on their wedding night, the daughters of Danaus have trouble finding new suitors; their father therefore decides to offer their hands in marriage without demanding an economic counterprovision *(hedna)* from the suitor. The provision will instead be athletic: the king has the suitors compete and distributes the princesses according to the results of the race.[73] Inspired by Danaus' actions, a certain Libyan, Pindar tells us, also decided to organize a race in order to choose a husband for his daughter. He placed her at the finish line, and the one who "succeed[ed] in touching the young girl's peplos first" became her husband.[74] To place one's hand on the young girl's peplos is here to prove oneself worthy of marrying her:

the symbolism of the garment is clear to all. The fabric is marriage. The interweaving of the virile warp and the feminine woof is a "myth" so strongly anchored in the collective memory that it requires no explanation. If upon reading Pindar's poem we consider the example of Danaus, who was ready to give his daughters in marriage in exchange for nothing and who thus furnished everything from his own treasure—nuptial garments included—we are led to conclude that the Libyan acted in a similar fashion, accepting the victor Alexidamos[75] under his own roof and under the wedding peplos of his daughter.

In Ithaca, Penelope's home is the house of Odysseus. In the absence of the king (whose fate is still unknown to her and who may be dead), the suitors are eager to marry the queen, for to marry the widow of Odysseus would ensure succession to the defunct king's throne.[76] To put off such a wedding, Penelope finds a pretext: for three years, she has been weaving a *pharos*. The suitors agree to await its completion, unaware of the fact that at night the queen undoes the work accomplished that day—until she is discovered and the suitors demand a decision.[77]

Recounted in this succinct fashion, Penelope's ruse suggests that the garment being woven and unraveled is that of her own wedding with one of the suitors, an event that is not as unthinkable as one might imagine, since according to other traditions the queen capitulated to one of the suitors, or even to all of them.[78] By weaving, she prepares her wedding; by undoing the fabric, she delays it—except that, according to Homer, the *pharos* in question is destined to bury Laertes the day he dies.[79] This curious explanation probably serves to absolve the queen of all suspicion of

THE CRAFT OF ZEUS

envisaging marriage to one of the suitors. For are we to believe that Laertes—this "opulent man"[80]—possessed no garment that might serve as a shroud?[81] Are we to believe that the suitors were ready to wait three years for the fabrication of anything but the nuptial garment destined for their own wedding? On the other hand, one might imagine that a version earlier than the *Odyssey* would have considered the eventual completion of the *pharos* as the coup de grâce for the father of Odysseus and that subsequently the garment became the old man's shroud (especially since, in dream interpretation, the completed cloth, detached from the loom, signifies death).[82] One might easily imagine Laertes saying to himself: "If she completes the *pharos*, it will be my death." If our hypothesis is correct, the *pharos* prepared by Penelope is of the sort that Hypsipyle furnishes for her wedding with Jason. Let us now attempt to confirm this.[83]

In his *Life of Romulus,* Plutarch tells how King Tarchetius, in order to punish his own daughter and her accomplice (a servant) for having disobeyed him, places the two young girls in prison. "Then he gave them a cloth to weave in their prison, promising that he would marry them once they had finished it."[84] To prepare for their own weddings, the young girls must complete the cloth. As in the case of Penelope, there will be no wedding without a nuptial blanket, to be furnished by her who will lie beneath it.[85] That is not all, however. For Plutarch continues: "But when they had woven all day, other women came, by order of Tarchetius, to unravel the cloth during the night."[86] Upon reading this passage, one cannot help but think of Penelope's famous ruse. It is our belief that we have here a traditional theme, anchored in custom, according to which an heiress weaves her own wedding blanket.

Up until now, our examples of union beneath the cloak have been conjugal and heterosexual in nature. The reason for this is simple: marriage seems to be the model that other types of union appropriate when attempting to define non-conjugal relationships as "marriages," whether with or without ironic intention. Thus, a long fragment by Archilochus, published in 1974, depicts a seducer and a young girl beneath a "nuptial" *chlaina*.[87] The poet speaks ill of Neoboulē in a discourse pronounced in the presence of her younger sister. After this he lays the graceful virgin among the flowers, "covering her with a soft *chlaina*."[88] There follows a detailed description of the lover's pleasures as he "caresses the pretty body"[89] of his prey. Here the seducer's covering of the young girl undoubtedly aims to suggest to her that their union is conjugal in nature, a lie by which the seduction is transformed into "nuptials" or "marriage." Realizing that the young girl would have preferred to wait for a real wedding, the lover suggests by his gesture that their union is the equivalent of a wedding, which is obviously not the case.[90]

The same pseudo-nuptial *chlaina* appears in several epigrams in the *Anthologia Palatina*, first in a poem by Meleager: "If someone, lying beneath Heliodora's cover [*hupo chlainei*], gets hot there, from the warmth of a flesh that staves off sleep, may the lamp go out, and may he, in the arms of the beauty who shakes him as she might, remain as motionless as a second Endymion."[91] No doubt Heliodora is a courtesan whose infidelity torments our man with jealousy of an eventual rival lying beside his beloved beneath this *chlaina* that, with each union that takes place beneath it, tends to make a "marriage." May every new "husband" of Heliodora resemble Endymion, since he, whose name we have translated as "the one of the garment," was ultimately able to do no more than sleep, eternally, beneath his blanket.

Another epigram by the same Meleager depicts the courtesan Demo; "O morning, why now, cruel to lovers, do you slowly unravel around the world, when another grows warm beneath the *chlanis* of Demo?"[92] The *chlanis*, which, according to Hesychius, is practically identical with the *chlaina*,[93] also covers a couple celebrating a fictitious wedding. On the other hand, we have no way of knowing whether this is the situation in a epigram by Asclepiades, which is important because of his use of the formula that we have already encountered in Theocritus: "For lovers, supreme happiness corresponds to the moment when the shared blanket [*mia . . . chlaina*] hides them and when Cypris is honored by both together."[94] It is impossible to say whether these "lovers" *(phileontes)* are husband and wife; the only reason to think that the "shared blanket" is nonconjugal here is the nature of the poems immediately surrounding it in the *Anthologia.*

Thus, the nuptial blanket—called *chlaina,* or even *mia chlaina*—can cover lovers who are not husband and wife, disguising their union as a "nuptial" or a "marriage." This gestural and semantic operation is also possible when lovers are of the same sex, as indicated by the story told by Alcibiades in Plato's *Symposium:* "So, without allowing him [Socrates] to say anything further, I got up and covered him with my own clothes [*himation*]—for it was winter—

and then laid myself down under his worn cloak [*tribōn*], and threw my arms round this truly superhuman and wonderful man, and remained thus the whole night."[95] Although the term *chlaina* is noticeably absent in this description of a "marriage" between men, it appears in one of the authors who returns to this anecdote, namely Athenaeus: "It is beneath the same blanket [*hupo tēn autēn chlaina*] that Socrates and Alcibiades slept together."[96] If the union of spouses beneath the same nuptial blanket constitutes the norm, it is thus possible to use the *chlaina* as a metaphor in several ways: it can signify the nonlawful union of a man and a woman as well as the "marriage" between two men, the lover *(erastēs)*, and the beloved *(eromenos)*, in this case united by a spiritual rather than a physical love. One might ultimately imagine that Sapphic love, both spiritual and physical, used the same symbolism of garments, despite the fact that this is not attested in the fragments. For amorous relations in Sappho's milieu are "conjugal" in nature: thus, we learn in one fragment that "Archeanassa is the spouse [*sundugos = suʒux*] of Gorgo."[97]

In order for this distinction between what we consider to be the norm and what appear to be derived, metaphorical forms to seem less arbitrary, we must find a context in which the vestimentary symbolism of legitimate marriage wins out over its "derived" forms. Pindar's first *Nemean Ode* presents us with such a situation. Hera is the lawful spouse of Zeus. Alcmena is only a mortal concubine, but not just any concubine, since she is the mother of Heracles (who later, in order to be adopted by Hera, must pass beneath the "garments," *endumata*, of the goddess).[98] As we can well imagine, the lawful wife is not pleased about the birth of the hero: "*Chrusothronos* Hera failed not to see him when he was swaddled in his saffron baby-clothes. The Queen of the Gods was angry at heart and at once sent snakes . . . But Heracles lifted his head on high and made his first trial of battle."[99] This combat sent terror through the chamber where Alcmena had just given birth: the women around the bed panicked, and the mother herself "unclothed [*apeplos*] as she was, jumped to her feet from her blankets and would ward off the arrogant brutes."[100] It is thus in vestimentary terms that Pindar chose to mark the difference between the lawful spouse and the concubine: Hera is "dressed with her cloak of golden flowers," Alcmena is "unclothed, without a peplos." Even though the union between Zeus and Alcmena took place beneath a "nuptial" garment (in the bed that the mother of Heracles normally shares with Amphitryon, her lawful spouse),[101] it is not a legitimate union: next to Hera, Alcmena cannot be considered Zeus's "spouse."

Another *ménage à trois*, found in Sophocles' *Women of Trachis*, can be briefly compared to this one. In her extreme despair, Deianeira imagines that beneath the "shared blanket" *(mias hupo chlainēs)*, in the company of her rival Iole, their shared spouse will take them in his arms.[102] By pushing Deianeira's imagination to this point—to the point of absurdity—Sophocles does not contradict the norm, which obviously requires that the husband, in this case Heracles, content himself with one lawful wife.

In the passage by Pindar, *chrusothronos* in any case defines the status of Hera, the lawful spouse, and *apeplos* that of the concubine. The same logic obtains in the use of another epithet for Hera, *prōtothronos*, in two late texts (from the fifth century): *Dionysiaca* by Nonnus and *The Rape of Helen* by Colluthus. Catching sight of Semele while she is bathing in the Aesopus river, Zeus is overcome by an irresistible desire to see "the entire white body" of the princess from up close.[103] He leaves the sky and approaches in order to "measure the naked body of the young girl."[104] Yet, continues the poet, "he thought that it wasn't enough just to *look* at the young unmarried girl [*azuga kourēn*]."[105] He therefore decides to climb into Semele's "nighttime bed" and impatiently await the apparition of the Evening Star.[106] Dionysos is conceived. The reaction of the lawful wife is predictable; it is pointless to go into detail, for a single observation suffices. In preparing her revenge, Hera is addressed as follows by Aphrodite: "Mother of Enyalius [that is, Ares], *prōtothronos* wife of Zeus!"[107] The emphasis on the naked body of Semele, the young unmarried girl, is offset by this definition of the lawful spouse as *prōtothronos*, "the one of the first *throna*" (we will soon return to the meaning of this vestimentary epithet).

As for the text by Colluthus, it brings into play the Judgment of Paris.[108] First Athena speaks, promising the young hero the courage of a warrior if he prefers her. Next Hera speaks and, in accordance with her status as the lawful spouse of Zeus Basileus, promises him the kingdom of Asia. The poet continues: "Such lordship did *prōtothronos* Hera offer to bestow. But Cypris lifted up her deep-bosomed robe [*heanon*] and bared her breast to the air and had no shame. And lifting with her hands the honeyed girdle of the Loves she bared all her bosom and heeded not her breasts."[109] What does she promise Paris then? "In place of manly prowess I will give thee a lovely bride, and, instead of kingship, enter thou the bed of Helen."[110] Once again, a *prōtothronos* Hera is opposed to feminine nudity, evocative of a nonlawful union. The status of Zeus's lawful wife is expressed by the vestimentary epithet.

Now, *prōtothronos* is also the epithet given Artemis in Callimachus' *Hymn* to her.[111] "Lady of many shrines, of many cities, hail!" exclaims Callimachus. "Goddess of the tunic [*chitōnē*], sojourner in Miletus . . . Lady of Chesion and of Imbrasus, *prōtothronos* . . ."[112] The parallelism between the two epithets is striking. Whereas Artemis is "goddess of the tunic" in Miletus, she is "the one of the first *throna*" in Samos. Not "the one of the first throne," as translators and commentators of the passage have it; in Samos, the "first throne" would certainly belong to Hera.[113] Instead, it is a vestimentary epithet, whose meaning we must now attempt to define.

First let us cite the lexicographer Pollux: "It is to Hera, as well as to Artemis and the Moirai, that young girls are vowed by preliminary wedding rituals [*proteleiais*]. On this occasion, the young girls offer their hair to these goddesses. She who is a virgin when she marries is called *prōtoposis* ('wife for the first time')."[114] This last remark in effect points the way to an understanding of the element *prōto-* in the epithet *prōtothronos*. If the second element is derived from *throna*, "flowered garments," the epithet must simply refer to the dress worn by the bride who is married for the first time, the dress that will also serve as a nuptial blanket. In her capacity as goddess of the first conjugal union, Hera is qualified by this epithet. According to the same logic, Aphrodite receives the epithet *prōtozux*, "of the first yoke, of the first sexual union," in an epigram from the *Antholo-*

gia Palatina.[115] Further, if Artemis is as *prōtothronos* as Hera, it is because she too, as shown by Pollux's citation, is connected to marriage: the virgin goddess prepares the young girl for her wedding. The Athenians even voted that it should be forbidden for a young girl to marry a man "if she has not served as a 'she-bear' to Artemis."[116] The young girl, then, cannot arrive at the wedding without passing by the goddess a virgin. No "first wedding dress" without her. Nor can the young girl celebrate her wedding without passing by Hera. In this way, it is under the protection of Artemis *prōtothronos* that the young girl arrives at her first wedding (by which she becomes a *prōtoposis*); from then on, she is under the protection of another *prōtothronos*, namely Hera, goddess of the first nuptials, of the first marriage. It is thus in the passage from the status of girl to that of married woman that Artemis encounters Hera, so to speak, both of them *prōtothronoi*.

In Pindar, as we have seen, Hera is *chrusothronos.* Yet this is not the only epithet of this sort that she receives from the Theban poet, who begins his eleventh *Nemean Ode* as follows: "Daughter of Rhea, to you the council hall belongs, Hestia, sister of highest Zeus and of *homothronos* Hera, receive Aritagoras gladly into your chamber!"[117] It seems perfectly conceivable to translate the epithet used here by "who shares her nuptial blanket," a translation that we have already attempted to justify at great length. It is true that Rhea is sitting on a *thronos* in the second *Olympian Ode,*[118] it is also true that the Charites—who wove Aphrodite's peplos[119]—have their *thronoi* on Olympus, according to the fourteenth *Olympian Ode.*[120] But given that none of the epithets ending in -*thronos* in Pindar requires the trans-

lation "sitting on the throne (of such or such a character),"
it is undoubtedly more reasonable to choose the vestimentary interpretation, especially since at times the translation
"sitting on a throne" becomes frankly absurd. Before con-
cluding, let us look at the remaining *chrusothronos*-type
epithets in Pindar.

The tenth *Nemean Ode* begins with the following invocation: "The city of Danaus and his fifty *aglaothronoi*
daughters, sing of it, Graces, of Argos, home of Hera, fit
for the gods!"[121] Should the consensus really be followed,
resulting in the translation "his fifty girls with their splendid
thrones"? We beg to differ. To align the fifty Danaids on
as many "thrones" is to ignore their status as young nubile
girls, first and foremost murderers of their husbands under
the nuptial covers (with the exception of Hypermestra,
mentioned a few lines later in the poem),[122] then offered
freely by Danaus to suitors qualified by an athletic competition.[123] It is clearly the *throna*, "flowered garments," of
the Danaids that are "splendid," not their "thrones." Let
us add a detail that may tend in the same direction. We
have suggested that the *Endumatia* in Argos was a festival
celebrating Hera's "investiture."[124] According to this hypothesis, the vestimentary epithet of the Danaids, which is
connected to their nuptials, unquestionably evokes an epithet such as *chrusothronos*, which is specific to Hera, particularly since the fighter celebrated by Pindar in the poem
that concerns us seems to have won not the Nemean Games
but the Argive Heraea[125] (= the *Endumatia?*).

Nothing prevents us from understanding the epithet
euthronoi, used in the second *Olympian Ode*, in the same
manner and from translating it as "with well-made, well-

woven *throna*."[126] The word is used there to characterize the daughters of Kadmos, in particular Semele and Ino. The note added by the French translator, Aimé Peuch, to the Belles Lettres edition, is significant: "Literally, *with beautiful thrones;* the epithet . . . is suited to a divinity who is seated in a temple; it indicates that the daughters of Kadmos were elevated to heroine, or, if one prefers, divine, status. I translated *glorious,* following Boissonade, to better indicate the meaning, which with a literal translation would remain too obscure." We are quoting this note because of its sincerity faced with a genuine difficulty. But instead of flattening *euthronoi* into "glorious," in our opinion one should return the vestimentary meaning to the epithet, the implications of which are by no means negligible, either in the case of Semele (as we have seen) or in the case of Ino, who became the wife of Athamas and whose veil *(krēdemnon)* would later save Odysseus from drowning.[127]

Let us quickly examine three other examples of *euthronos,* qualifying Aphrodite, the Seasons, and Clio, respectively. In the second *Isthmian,* mention is made of a boy "whose glorious summer recalls *euthronos* Aphrodite."[128] Goddess of amorous union, Aphrodite is also the goddess of the blanket beneath which lovers unite, whether or not their union is lawful or heterosexual (in this sense, she differs from Hera). The vestimentary meaning is thus preferable here. More ambiguous is the example of the *euthronoi* Seasons, who, in the ninth *Pythian,*[129] are entrusted with Aristaeus, the child of Apollo and of the nymph Cyrene. For they in fact take the child "on their knees," *epigounidion,*[130] which presupposes a seated position. That said, the poet is obviously not obliged to explain, by an epithet, the seated position of someone who takes an infant onto his knees; and it is perhaps more important to note that the person in question is dressed in rich clothing. (Indeed, the Seasons are experts in matters of clothing: we have seen that they participated in the fabrication of the peplos worn by Aphrodite).[131] Finally, the third example of *euthronos*, in the third *Nemean Ode*, offers little more to the interpreter: the epithet qualifies the Muse Clio.[132] Nonetheless, there is no need to translate it as "seated on a well-made throne"; the translation "dressed in beautiful flowered garments" is not at all out of keeping with the context.[133]

The same remark is more or less valid for the epithet qualifying the Muses in the thirteenth *Olympian Ode*, namely *aglaothronoi*.[134] But it is reasonable to think that the meaning of the word is the same as in the second *Olympian Ode*, where we concluded in favor of the vestimentary meaning (the Danaids "dressed in splendid robes"). On the other hand, another epithet, *hupsithronos*, used first to qualify one of the Moirai, namely Clotho,[135] then the Nereids, in particular Thetis,[136] seems to pose a real problem. For a "raised throne" is easy to imagine, while a "high" garment is not. Here a gloss by Hesychius comes to our aid: although it may be difficult to translate, the adjective *hupsistolos* is unquestionably vestimentary.[137] We propose taking the element *hupsi-* as indicating the vertical breadth, so to speak, of the garment (remember that *bathu-* and *busso-*, "deep," can have a comparable meaning).[138]

Here is one last case of an epithet ending in -*thronos*. When, in the ninth *Pythian Ode*, Pindar celebrates the victory of Telesikrates of Cyrene, he recounts the love and the wedding *(gamos)* of Apollo and the nymph Cyrene, the parents of Aristaeus: "In Libya's rich golden room they lay together."[139] Here the wealth of the site of their union is emphasized, the wealth of the city of Cyrene. On the other hand, when in the fourth *Pythian Ode* the poet returns briefly to Cyrene, it is to emphasize not the wealth of her *home* but that of her *garment:* "After that Lato's son gave you Libya's plain, for the Gods love you, to enrich and govern the holy city of *chrusothronos* Cyrene."[140] Why is Cyrene "dressed in golden *throna*"? Obviously, this epithet evokes the wealth of her city. But having celebrated a wedding with Apollo, she also bears the epithet in memory of her union with the god. She "married well," one might say. This was also the case of another wife of Apollo, Coronis. But instead of remaining faithful to the god, whose child she was already carrying, she married a mortal: "Like that was the great blindness of the soul," says Pindar in the third *Pythian*, "of *kallipeplos* Coronis. For a stranger came from Arcadia, and she lay in his bed: but the watcher saw her."[141] While the epithet *tanupeplos* (Helen) indicated the meaning of *chrusothronos* (Hera),[142] the parallel between Coronis *kallipeplos* and Cyrene *chrusothronos* is also striking. Coronis and Cyrene both "married well." They are the wives of the same god and will give birth to Asclepius and Aristaeus, respectively. It seems reasonable to assume, as in the cases of Helen and Hera, that their vestimentary epithets symbolize their status as wives—which one ultimately betrays while the other does not.

In conclusion, let us step outside the purely nuptial, conjugal, or erotic framework. For if *throna* signifies "garments with flowered designs," as asserted by Kleitarchos,[143] this meaning relates not only to the interpretation of the epithets ending in -*thronos*—a large number of which are, in our opinion, vestimentary in nature—but also to the classification of lyric poetry. For under the entry *Pindaros* in the *Suda*, we read that the poet wrote *Enthronismoi*, among other things. This is normally translated as "Enthronements," without questioning whether there existed ritual occasions in antique society during which someone was put on the "throne." When would they occur?[144] Now, the examination of epithets ending in -*thronos* in Pindar indicated to us that the poet was sensitive to the vestimentary significance of *throna*. This is why we propose the translation "Investitures" for his *Enthronismoi*, a translation that has the advantage of fitting easily into the cultural reality. For a poetic composition titled *enthronismos* is obviously likely to accompany "investitures" (still in the literal meaning) of cult statues, such as those we encountered in Elis, Athens, Sparta, and Argos.[145] One can easily imagine a type of chant commissioned specifically for *peplophoria*.[146] Moreover, we know that a book entitled *Thronismoi mētroioi* was attributed to Orpheus.[147] How are we to understand this title, so similar to the Pindaric *Enthronismoi?* We propose "Investitures of the Mother" (or "Maternal Garments"), invoking in support another title of an Orphic book, *Peplos,* which is clearly garment-related,[148] as well as the existence of a substantive that is parallel to *thronismos* (< *throna*), namely *himatismos* (< *himation*), signifying "garment."[149] Lexically, we may also note the existence of the verb *enchlainōomai* ("I am dressed in"),[150] parallel to *enthronizomai,* which seems to indicate that the vestimentary meaning is formally acceptable for the word *Enthronismoi*. In this somewhat unexpected manner, we have in fact reconnected with our point of departure, political weaving in Elis, with which the Elean exegesis also associated the union of the bride and groom. Between civic and nuptial fabrics, there is in reality a relationship of the deepest sort.

4

THE MARRIAGE OF
PELEUS AND THETIS:
NUPTIAL BLANKETS
IN ROME

IT IS THANKS to a twenty-page article published in 1928 that today we can place the nuptial garment squarely at the center of the symbolism of Roman marriage; indeed, the content of the classic study by Margherita Guarducci[1] has never been surpassed by subsequent studies;[2] for although primarily iconographic inquiries into symbolic garments, nuptial or otherwise, have considerably enriched our knowledge of the material facts, no true progress has since been made regarding the interpretation of acts involving garments. Guarducci's three conclusions, which are based in part on a study by G. F. Gamurrini (1889),[3] seem to be the only ones worth noting and appear, rightfully, in later studies.

Guarducci's point of departure is an Etruscan funerary urn dating from the sixth century B.C. and now at the Museum of Chiusi.[4] Although the lower part of the vessel is damaged, the images that figure on its four sides are essentially recognizable. Two of them are related to weddings: on one of the shorter sides, we see a *coemptio*, the ritual "purchase" of the future wife; one of the long sides—and this is the one that is of interest to us—depicts a marriage procession, led by an *aulos* player, proceeding from right to left. Behind the musician comes a priest wearing a pointed hat. Looking backward, the young man who follows is wearing a crown like the *aulos* player but is carrying a branch in his hand. Following these figures is a group of five individuals, two of whom—a man to the left, a woman to the right—hold a wide piece of fabric over the heads of the other three, who are engaged in the ritual of *manu captio*, by which the groom violently "seizes" the bride by the arm, thereby signifying that he is taking possession of her. The couple beneath the cloth is assisted by a woman who, according to Guarducci, is the mother of the bride surrendering her daughter to the groom. The "cover" is thus spread over the couple to be married, but not as it is in Greek documents. Although it is covering them during a particularly important moment in the wedding, it is not the moment of sexual union. Rather the moment seems more symbolic or conceptual, even legal, in nature.

In late Greek, this kind of nuptial cloth is called *pastos*,[5] a word derived form the verb *passein*, which we have already encountered in the passage of the *Iliad* in which Andromache "sprinkles" *(epasse)* her cloth with embroidered flowers.[6] Yet rather than a bedcover, the Greek *pastos* seems to be a fabric hung over the nuptial bed. The Chiusi urn represents a different type of situation: the fabric is held over the bride and groom while they are standing rather than in bed, surrounded by people who are indispensable to the proper realization of the *manu captio*. Putting aside the purely nuptial setting for a moment to ascertain the significance of this cloth, Guarducci cites a fragment from Aristotle's *Customs of the Tyrrhenians:* "The Tyrrhenians dine in the company of their wives, lying beneath the same cloak [*hupo tōi autlōi himatiōi*]."[7] Unlike the Greeks, who eat their meals without their wives, the Etruscans may dine together on condition that the couple is covered by a single cloak: it is the couple as a unit that is lying on the table-couch, rather than two individuals. We might add to Guarducci's analysis that this cloak could hardly be the *metonymic* figure of the physical "interlacing" of the spouses, as it could be for the Greeks (among whom, according to a scholiast, the *chlaina* represents *koitē,* that is, the "cloak," "the nuptial bed");[8] it is the *metaphor* for their unity. The cloth is union. In other words, holding a cloth over the bride and groom is not so much an evocation of its practical usage as is the blanket on the nuptial bed; it also and most importantly signifies by a ritual gesture the close union on many levels of the bride and groom beneath it. Later, well after the wedding, the garment covering the couple during a meal will continue to bear this significance, marking the bond between the two spouses lying at the table and distinguishing them from the other guests.

The second image studied by Guarducci is a fragment of a temple pediment dating from the second century B.C. and found in Civitalba, a small site situated a few dozen kilometers east of Gubbio.[9] At the center of the pediment, the sculptor represented the marriage of Dionysos and

Ariadne. This part is now lost. What remains is the "frame," as Guarducci calls it, two winged nude figures holding a large cloak behind the bride and groom. Thus in this artifact a cloak is situated behind the bride and groom rather than above them. In the Greek tradition this cloak *(peplos)* was among the gifts offered to Jason by Hypsipyle: in book 4 of the *Argonautica,* Apollonius Rhodius states that it was the work of the Charites and had been passed on from Dionysos to Thoas, who in turn had given it to the queen of Lemnos.[10] A marvel to touch *(aphassein)* and to behold *(eishoran),* this cloak bore the nectarous perfume with which Dionysos had saturated it when he slept beneath it *(enkatēlekto)* with Ariadne.[11]

Leaving the Etruscan domain behind, Guarducci devotes the second part of her article to the wedding representations on Roman sarcophagi, in particular those of the imperial period.[12] According to these images, on the day of the wedding, after the nuptial *consensus,* the Roman bride and groom performed the *dextrarum iunctio:* they "joined" their right hands, exchanging vows and invoking Juno Pronuba ("Nuptial"),[13] among other divinities. Now, quite frequently this ritual was performed beneath or in front of a large piece of luxurious fabric, the *aulaeum.* In this nuptial textile Guarducci is inclined to recognize "if not the living continuation, at least something very close to the large cloak of Etruscan monuments."[14] In support of her thesis, she invokes a lexical fact that is difficult to dispute. In classical Latin the verb *nubere* means "to marry," with the restriction that it is said only of the woman.[15] But this restriction is recent: "The ancients said *nubere* not only for women who married but also for men, as the Italics still

THE CRAFT OF ZEUS

do," writes the erudite Nonius Marcellus in the third century.[16] Now, *nubere* comes from the root *nub-*, which also produced the substantive *nubes*, "cloud,"[17] and the verb *obnubilare*, "to obnubilate."[18] In addition to the abstract sense of "to marry," *nubere* thus possesses a concrete meaning, "to cover." If in classical Latin *nubere* is used only for the woman, the reason is undoubtedly that she is the one who "covers herself" with her veil, the *flammeum*, for the wedding ceremony. At a certain period the Romans preferred to add the concrete meaning of *nubere* to this nuptial veil, reserved for the woman, which brought about an analogous restriction in the abstract use of the verb. But before that, *nubere* could also be said of men: this linguistic fact seems to have been depicted on the urn of Chiusi and on the facade of Civitalba. "They are covered, therefore they are marrying." The meaning of the term *conubium*, "marriage," is even more precise: the prefix *co-* indicates that the bride and groom are "together" beneath the "cover." The epithet of Juno invoked by the couple "beneath the cover," namely *Pronuba*, can be understood in the same way: the *nuptial* goddess is necessarily the goddess of the "cover" of the bride and groom.

What is the significance of the fact that the bride and groom are thus "covered" or *nupti?* Guarducci proposes the three conclusions to which we alluded earlier: (1) originally the common veil "isolated" the ritual and thereby consecrated the matrimonial union; (2) thereafter it became the symbol of the indissoluble bond between the husband and wife; (3) at the same time, it could signify the protection offered by the husband to the wife.[19] Consecration, union, protection: we will not deny that these three meanings attributed to the nuptial cloak are reasonable, but it should be emphasized that they are more intuitive or descriptive than analytical in nature. From a more practical standpoint we must ask ourselves what the logic is that allows the myth of the nuptial cloak "covering" the bride and groom to function among the Etruscans and the Romans. If common sense tells us that Guarducci is right to see this cloak as the symbol of *union*, how can we grasp the logic of this symbol? The reader will not be surprised if we respond by proposing the model of the interweaving of the warp and the woof, the interlacing of sexually dissimilar threads, which we have studied so extensively in the Greek context. In our opinion, what makes fabric the symbol, or "myth," of marriage, are precisely these material properties, transformed into metaphors of conjugal relations—in Greece as well as in Italy. For although the Etruscan cloak and the Roman *aulaeum* are not objects that metonymically evoke the union of the spouses in the nuptial bed (as does Dionysos' *peplos* or Jason's *pharos*),[20] they are certainly metaphorical objects, the interlacing of whose threads signify union. The cloak is the metaphor for marriage. Or rather, it *is* the marriage.

This assertion is true on condition that the symbolism in question is attested among the Etruscans and the Romans. Now, the presence on Italic soil of the metaphor of the "interweaving" of the warp and woof—of the *sumplokē* of the *stēmōn* and *krokē*, to use the Greek terms—is unquestionable: one particularly unambiguous text in this regard, a text to which we referred earlier, is Seneca's *Letters to Lucilius*. In the text of the Roman writer, a contemporary of Nero, the Greek theory in the matter reappears, dressed in Latin terms: "Here is Posidonius, one of the men to whom philosophy is, in my opinion, most indebted: he first describes how one *twists* certain threads, how one *pulls up* others, soft and irregular skein, how then the canvas [*tela*], with the help of hanging weights, is pulled into a straight warp [*stamen*], how the woof [*subtemen*], introduced to soften the tension of the warp [*tramae (sic)*] that squeezes it on both sides, is forced to couple with it [*coire cogatur*] and to be married to it [*iungi*] by the pressure of the blade [*spatha*]; he concludes by crediting the wise man with the very invention of the weaver's technique, forgetting that a more ingenious system has since been discovered."[21] Hereafter Seneca pursues the subject of weaving further, describing the competition between Minerva and Arachne in Ovid and the fabrication of transparent garments, before passing without transition to his next topic, namely the invention of agriculture.[22] In weaving, he writes, one introduces the woof in order to constrain it to "unite sexually" with the warp. Although Seneca cannot render in Latin the gender of the Greek terms of weaving—the masculine warp, the feminine woof—he compensates for this handicap by the rather crude expression used to designate the interlacing of the threads. To cross the threads is to couple them. The interlacing of the warp thread (*stamen*, neuter) and the woof thread (*subtemen*, also neuter) is coitus. We understand then why the nuptial canvas held over the heads of the bride and groom does not need to be placed on the nuptial bed in order to signify the union of the spouses: it can do so autonomously, held in the air by "persons of honor" during the *dextrarum iunctio,* since it constitutes in itself a sexual union.

Thus the nuptial cloth, unifying by interlacing the warp and the woof, is central to the Etruscan and Roman *conubium,* since it ensures the intelligibility of the matrimonial union. The *conubium* is the passage of the bride and groom under the same woven cloth. Beneath this fabric, the idea of the union can be seen and touched. (The *dextrarum iunctio* that takes place under the cloth only repeats the "chiasma," or the crossing, of the warp and the woof.) Now, the Roman woman had this logic of marriage at the tip of her fingers, since we know that her principal activity was working with wool. We shall therefore now turn our attention to the *lanifica,* the woman "involved in wool work," paying special heed to the three weaver women of strategic importance in the Roman mind: Tanaquil, the "flaminica" (the wife of the *flamen Dialis*), and finally, the unfortunate Queen Dido.

Tanaquil, *summa lanifica,* "the spinner of spinners," is for the Romans the main figure of wool work.[23] A passage in Pliny the Elder's *Natural History* gives us details about this spinner, who also turns out to be a weaver: "Marcus Varro informs us, on his own authority, that the wool on the distaff and spindle of Tanaquil (who was also called Gaia Caecilia) was still preserved in the temple of Sancus; and also in the shrine of Fortune a pleated royal robe [*togam regiam*] made by her, which had been worn by Servius Tullius. Hence arose the practice that maidens at their marriage were accompanied by a decorated distaff and a spindle with thread. Tanaquil first wove a straight tunic [*prima texuit rectam tunicam*] of the kind that novices [*tirones*] wear with the plain white toga, and newly married brides [*nouaeque nuptae*]."²⁴

Tanaquil was the wife of the good King Tarquin the Elder, by whom she had two sons who were as dissimilar in nature as the warp and the woof: the older one, named Tarquin like his father, was given the nickname Superbus ("proud") because of his violent character; the younger son, on the contrary, was particularly gentle in nature.²⁵ Now, Tanaquil also had a servant woman named Ocrisia. One day she dressed her as a bride [*numphē*], and Ocrisia united with a phallus sprung from the cinders of the hearth, after which she gave birth to Servius Tullius, whose father was said to be the god Vulcan.²⁶ Upon the death of her husband the king, Tanaquil preferred Servius to her own sons as successor to the throne, even though he was little inclined to take power (a bit in the tradition of the good King Numa).²⁷ Servius nonetheless became an excellent king; he and his wife Gegania had two daughters, the elder (who, according to Plutarch, was also named Tanaquil)²⁸ every bit as gentle as the younger one, named Tullia, was violent. In keeping with Plato's logic of interlacing the "courageous" and the "moderate," which we studied at some length earlier, the future Tarquin the Proud should obviously have married the gentle daughter of Servius Tullius, and the violent Tullia should have married the "gentle" son of Tarquin the Elder and of Tanaquil. This in fact was the parents' plan, and so it came to pass until one day the two violent natures united and murdered their respective spouses, whereupon the old Servius Tullius was also assassinated. Finally Tarquin the Proud could take the throne: a pyrrhic victory, as one might well imagine, for the moral of the story is that he turned out to be the last king of Rome.

It would hardly be acceptable to introduce the theory of the weaver king, developed by Plato in *The Statesman*, into the story of the final kings of Rome if it were not for the fact that weaving plays a major role in the careers of both Tanaquil and Servius Tullius. Tanaquil dressed Ocrisia as a bride, no doubt by weaving her a *tunica recta* (which she was the first to weave); later, she would weave the *toga regia* for Servius Tullius,[29] which apparently had not only a concrete significance but also an abstract one, preparing her protégé's accession to the throne. And Servius Tullius himself, who had a privileged relationship with Fortuna, dedicated a statue to her which he covered in *togae praetextae*. According to Pliny, the *praetextae* of Fortune were preserved intact for 560 years.[30] Thus there was a *single* investiture of the cult statue; the solid construction of the fabric ensured that it would not need to be replaced. In our opinion it is highly significant that Tanaquil's weaving, like that of the Sixteen Women of Elis, had a double orientation: matrimonial for the occasion of Ocrisia's nuptials, political for the accession to power of the latter's son. In Rome these two orientations were therefore related: political weaving "descended" from matrimonial weaving, just as Servius Tullius descended from Ocrisia. As we stated earlier, a profound relationship exists between political and nuptial weaving.

Although the function of the King-Archon in Athens was not that of a real king, it nonetheless carried certain cult elements that must have been the prerogatives of the kings of an earlier period (we have assumed that it was he who dressed the statue of Athena Polias on the Acropolis every four years.)[31] In Rome the function of the *flamen Dialis* also bore the mark of institutions preceding the advent of the republic. Representative of the sovereign god, the "flamen of Jupiter" was the highest priest in Rome.[32] He lived in a particularly close relationship to his wife: if the *flaminica Dialis* died, the flamen had to leave his function.[33] Now, the main activity of the flaminica was working with wool, or, more specifically, weaving the cloak that her husband, like an ancient king, would wear constantly: "In the ancient pontifical religion," writes Servius, "it was stated that the garment worn for the consecration of the flamen and referred to as the *laena* had to be woven by the flaminica [*a flaminica texi oportere*]."[34] In this respect the flaminica is highly reminiscent of Queen Tanaquil weaving the *toga regia* of Servius Tullius. At the same time she is also the model of the Roman wife, the *domiseda*, spending her days spinning and weaving in the family home, near the conjugal bed.[35]

Varro derives the word *laena* from *lana*, "wool," on the basis of the fact that the garment thus designated had "as much wool as two togas combined."[36] Paul the Deacon in turn derives it from the Greek *chlaina*, "cloak,"[37] a term with which we have already developed some familiarity. Servius in turn considers the *laena* to be related to the cognomen Laenas used by the Popilii, descendants of Venus (the most famous member of whom, Caius Popilius Laenas, assassinated Cicero), and specifies the erotic aspect of the garment in question: "Some assert that it is a feminine garment, made for the lover as it were."[38] Again, the political or royal meaning of the garment coexists perfectly with the erotic sense.

Servius wrote the scholium just cited apropos of a passage in book 4 of the *Aeneid*, in which another royal weaver takes center stage. In this book the love of Dido and Aeneas is consummated and brought to an end. Juno Pronuba is at the origin of a remarkable hunting scene, during which a storm breaks that forced Aeneas and Dido to retreat, alone, into a grotto where their union occurs: "Primal Earth and Juno Pronuba give their sign," writes Virgil; "fires flashed in Heaven, the witness of their *conubia*, and on the mountain-top screamed the Nymphs."[39] *Conubia* which King Iarbas, who had unsuccessfully asked for the queen's hand in marriage, witnesses bitterly. Furious, he calls on Jupiter, who immediately sends Mercury to Aeneas to remind him of his destiny in Italy. When the messenger god arrives, "he sees Aeneas founding towers and building new houses. And lo! his sword was starred with yellow jasper, and a *laena* hung from his shoulders ablaze with Tyrian purple—a gift [*munera*] that wealthy Dido had wrought, interweaving the web [*telas*] with thread of gold."[40] Called to order, Aeneas immediately arouses Dido's suspicion, who implores him to stay—"by our marriage, by the wedlock begun [*per conubia nostra, per inceptos hymenaeos*],"[41] exclaims the unhappy weaver.

Aeneas, who had been welcomed into the queen's palace, was not at home: therefore, for his nuptials with Dido, over which the Pronuba presided in person, he was not the one to furnish the nuptial cover, at least if we assume that Greek custom prevailed in the *Aeneid*. And we do indeed have the impression that the *laena* worn by Aeneas was the equivalent of the Greek *mia chlaina* ("shared cover"). Because she received her spouse in her own home, Dido offered him the nuptial *laena*, her own handiwork, which the hero would wear in memory of their wedding, just as Jason wore the *pharos* offered by Hypsipyle. During their first union in the grotto, one might imagine, Dido and Aeneas were covered by this nuptial *laena*. Was it therefore a "Greek-style" union? No doubt; but with certain "Roman-style" nuances. The myth of weaving, generator of the diverse and at times divergent representations that we have studied, remained the same in Rome as in Greece, which made the Roman appropriation of the Greek representations we are considering extremely easy. On both sides, the fabric is a marriage.

One of these representations is the mythical story of the union of Peleus and Thetis. In the sumptuous version given by Catullus in his *Poems* 64,[42] the fabric beneath which the hero and the goddess are to celebrate their nuptials is literally given center stage: "But see, the royal marriage bed is being set for the goddess in the midst of the palace [*sedibus in mediis*] . . . covered with purple [*purpura*] tinged with the rosy stain of the shell. This coverlet *(uestis)*, broidered with shapes of ancient men, with wondrous art sets forth the worthy deeds of heroes."[43] If, on this level, the poet accords a central place to the nuptial fabric, situated "in the midst of the palace," the description of the same garment occupies a no less significant, indeed an almost overwhelming place, on the level of the text; of the 408 lines in the poem, 215 are devoted to the *uestis* of the nuptial bed.[44] What are the "worthy deeds of heroes" this veil retraces? It depicts the tragic story of Ariadne, abandoned by Theseus on the shores of the island of Dia. Strictly speaking, the description, or *ekphrasis*, of the fabric does not occupy this entire long passage but more specifically $24 + 83 = 107$ lines,[45] which portray the heroine on the deserted beach at the moment when she "sees Theseus as he sails away with swift fleet."[46] This is the point of departure for the poet, who recounts the entire history of the couple, from the beginning until Theseus' return to Athens, before returning to the "real" subject of his poem, the wedding of Peleus and Thetis.[47]

On the nuptial cloth, spread on the bed, we see a desperate Ariadne, "with streaming eyes . . . like a marble figure of a bacchanal."[48] Separated forever from the man with whom she has just celebrated her *conubia*,[49] she allows herself to be stripped naked by the wind. Her veil *(amictus)* slides off her body and is carried away by the waves. She is no longer concerned with it. "It was to you, Theseus," says Catullus, "that all her heart, her soul, her spirit clung in her bewilderment."[50] Thus, the wife of the hero (qualified as *coniunx* in line 123) appears here uncovered, nude, at the very moment when, in keeping with her status as bride, she should have been "covered" by a fabric. In her very person, she incarnates in some sense the contradiction that we observed in Pindar, between the legitimate wife *chrusothronos* and the concubine *apeplos*.[51] Ariadne's appearance, of course, gives the poet the occasion to evoke nudity in its aesthetic dimension (comparison with the marble statue of a maenad), but it is also, and mainly, legible on a sociological level: the nuptials are transformed into their own negation. Thus the image that furnishes him with a pretext immediately situates the story of Ariadne and Theseus within a solidly nuptial problematic, since the fabric destined to *cover* Peleus and Thetis depicts a *wife disrobed*. Ariadne's nudity signifies her separation from her spouse.

The story begins in Athens. To atone for the murder of Androgeus, the son of Minos, the Athenians are forced to send regular shipments of young boys and girls to Crete to be devoured by the Minotaur. Theseus, finding these "death convoys" intolerable, decides to accompany one by joining the ranks of the young Athenians and traveling to the home of Minos. Shortly after his arrival in the royal palace, the princess Ariadne sees Theseus and falls in love. She gives him the thread *(filum)* that will guide his steps *(uestigia)* to the exit of the Labyrinth after he has killed the Minotaur, who is the brother of the princess herself. Once the deed is done, Ariadne leaves Crete (and her father, sister, and mother) to follow Theseus to Dia, where their wedding is celebrated. Upon awaking from their night of love, the young princess realizes that her husband has left her. This is the story that Catullus recounts, in a flashback,[52] to situate the image woven into the cover of the nuptial bed.

Next it is Ariadne who speaks, reproaching Theseus, in a long monologue,[53] for having abandoned her contrary to his promises: "This was not what you led me to expect with all my heart, but rather a joyful union and a marriage that would surpass my greatest desires [*sed conubia laeta, sed optatos hymenaeos*]."[54] (Dido was to repeat the essence of this statement in the *Aeneid*, as we have seen.)[55] Unlike Theseus, twice qualified as "forgetful" *(immemor)*,[56] Ariadne has sacrificed everything: "When you were turning in the whirl [*turbo*] of death, I tore you from it, choosing to cause the death of my brother rather than fail you, traitor, at the moment of truth."[57] Now, on the desert island, she will fall prey to savage beasts. She continues: "If your heart rejected the thought of our union because you feared the inhuman authority of your old father, at least you could have led me to your home; I would have been happy to serve as your slave, to bathe your white feet [*uestigia*] in limpid water or to spread your bed with a purple coverlet [*purpurea . . . ueste*]."[58] The purple coverlet of which Ariadne is thinking is thus not that of her own nuptial bed but one that would cover Theseus and another wife. By a cruel irony, she reminds us of the one that is placed on the joyous bed of Peleus and Thetis: *purpura . . . uestis.*[59] Ariadne's only recourse in this situation is the Eumenides, who avenge her unhappiness. Ariadne concludes: "Since Theseus was forgetful enough to abandon me to this solitude, O goddesses, may a similar forgetfulness bring misfortune to him and his own!"[60] Her prayer will be granted.

And by intermediary of a cloth. For Theseus forgets not only the "nuptial cloth," with all its implications, thereby making Ariadne's separation from her father a tragic one, but also another cloth, thus causing the death of his own father. Twice he forgets a cloth, causing two symmetrical separations. For before allowing his son to leave for Crete, Aegeus had dark sails raised on the ship that was to lead the young people to an almost certain death; but if, against all expectations, Theseus succeeded in killing the Minotaur, Aegeus had instructed him: "As soon as you come within sight of our hills, I want your yardarms to cast off their funerary garments [*funestam . . . uestem*] and to raise on solid cables white sails [*candida . . . uela*], so that instantly upon seeing them I will have the pleasure of recognizing this happy signal when the blessed day of your return is here."[61] However, Catullus continues, "these orders, though at first faithfully retained by Theseus, escaped his memory . . . Glimpsing the swollen sails, his father threw himself from the rocky peak, believing that a cruel destiny had robbed him of his Theseus."[62] And thus "the victorious Theseus felt a sorrow equal to that which his forgetful heart had inflicted on the daughter of Minos."[63]

But this is not all: we have not yet depleted the vestimentary register of the story. For according to Catullus, Theseus was received as a "guest" *(hospes)* in the palace of Minos[64] and not as an enemy. According to Philochorus, quoted by Plutarch, Minos even organized games, and the king was reportedly quite pleased to see Theseus emerge the victor.[65] In fact it was during these games that Ariadne fell in love with the young hero.[66] Whatever the case may have been, Theseus' future wife received the hero in her own home[67]—just as Hypsipyle received Jason in her home, or as Dido received Aeneas in Carthage. If our theory is correct, this situation made it her responsibility to furnish the nuptial cloak; at least this would have been the expectation established by the tradition. Yet what does the princess offer her future *coniunx?* Not a fabric, a cloak or a coverlet. Because of the circumstances—for it is a matter of saving his life and ensuring his exit from the Labyrinth—she can give him only a "thread," a *filum.*[68] Catullus doesn't say so, but we know that it was the ingenious architect of the Labyrinth, Daedalus himself, who suggested this solution to her.[69] This "thread" is called *mitos* in the fifth-century B.C. historian Pherekydes and *stamen* in Propertius; both words mean "warp."[70] The thread offered to Theseus by Ariadne is thus a thread destined to fulfill the "male" function. Rolled into a ball, it makes a spiral shape, analogous to the "whirl" *(turbo)* of the Labyrinth itself.[71] Indeed, the ball will be unraveled by Theseus right into the heart of the Labyrinth; once he has killed the Minotaur, the hero will follow this same thread to find the exit. The ball borrows the shape of the Labyrinth as it is unrolled.[72]

By offering a thread to Theseus at the moment when their relationship would have called for the offering of a fabric, Ariadne in some sense made their union impossible. For this thread is destined to traverse the Labyrinth without crossing other threads—or in any case without crossing any threads other than itself. Unlike the *domus* where Peleus and Thetis unite, neither the royal palace nor the Labyrinth will unite the "loves" of Ariadne and Theseus into a "fabric."[73] For a thread is not a fabric. Thus despite its usefulness to Theseus, Ariadne's thread already symbolizes the couple's disunion and has the same implications as the garment that slips from the body of the princess in the scene represented on the tapestry of Peleus and Thetis. In fact one might say that the tragedy of Ariadne can be summarized as the choice between the thread, which would save Theseus, and the fabric, which would have retained him at the cost of his life.

This interpretation is corroborated by the fact that the Labyrinth, a site that is more "symbolic" than "architectural" (to adopt the terms used by Françoise Frontisi),[74] is a space associated with weaving: "As of old in high Crete 'tis said the Labyrinth held a path woven [*textum . . . iter*] with blind walls, and a bewildering work of craft with a thousand ways, where the tokens of the course were confused by the indiscoverable and irretraceable maze: even in such a course do the Trojan children entangle [*impediunt*] their steps, weaving [*texunt*] in sport their flight and conflict."[75] Now, if the Labyrinth traversed by Theseus is a space that exists under the sign of the "textile," the fabric that Theseus begins there cannot be finished: you cannot weave with a single thread. Indeed, two kinds, two *genres*, of thread are necessary, warp and woof, nubile boys and girls.

On its way back to Crete, Theseus' ship makes a stop at Delos. This is an episode that Catullus' *ekphrasis* omits, for the simple reason that the poet's story is centered upon the figure of Ariadne, who, by the time the young Athenians arrive at Delos, has already been left behind by her forgetful young husband. Nevertheless, because the episode at Delos is of capital importance in interpreting the thread in the Labyrinth, we shall put aside Catullus' text for the moment.

What happened at Delos that was so important? Let us read the key passage in Plutarch: "Theseus, upon his return to Crete, set down in Delos, and after sacrificing to the god and dedicating the statue of Aphrodite that Ariadne had given him, he performed a dance chorus [*echoreuse . . . choreian*] with the young people that they say is still practiced today among the Delians, and whose movements imitated [*mimema*] the twists and turns of the Labyrinth, on a punctuated rhythm of alternating, spiral-like movements [*parallaxeis kai anelixeis*]. The Delians give this kind of dance the name 'Crane' [*Geranos*], according to Dicaearchus. Theseus danced it around the Keraton, an alter made of horns [*kerata*], which are all left horns."[76] An invention of Daedalus—builder of the Labyrinth[77]—this dance is also "woven," according to a scholium to the *Iliad*.[78] Like the *lusus Troiae*, whose movements Virgil compares to the "woven" paths of the Labyrinth, the *Geranos* is characterized by interlaced movements.

Now, as we know, cranes fly in a delta formation (a letter whose invention was inspired by these birds,[79] except that one must picture it here as open at the bottom, like an upside-down V), a fact that is key to reconstructing the way in which this dance was executed. The second important element is of course the "woven" nature of the dance. The third element is only implicit in the story but is emphasized by Eustathius, according to whom the *Geranos* led by Theseus[80] was remarkable for the following reason: boys and girls danced in it *anamix*, together.[81] If the crane, as Aristotle says, is a bird that touches the two extremes of the world (namely the North and the South),[82] one might imagine that the name *Geranos* suggests that the dance at Delos touched the two "extremes" of the city, namely the masculine and the feminine, especially since the boys and the girls who danced it would soon become the first citizens of Athens.

At the beginning, then, a row of boys and a row of girls assume a delta formation. These two rows cross one another at the point where they meet—first advancing as a Δ, then forming an X and ultimately a V (an upside-down Δ). To "retie the knot" *(plekein)*, the dancers merely continue, turning slightly toward the interior and crossing one another again, each row now finding itself at the other's original place.[83] Another possibility is that the respective rows execute a semicircular movement which enables each to return, in the reverse direction, on the steps of the other. That this "weaving" took place around an altar of Apollo made of horns is hardly surprising. Even though Callimachus wishes us to believe that these are goat horns "woven" together by Apollo,[84] they are more suggestive of the half-bull image of the Minotaur, placed at the intersection of the "woven" paths of his home, paths that the *Geranos* is meant to imitate.

"After the death of Aegeus," writes Plutarch, "Theseus conceived of a grand and marvelous scheme: he gathered the inhabitants of Attica in a single city [*sunōikise . . . eis hen astu*] and made a single city for a single people . . . He give the city the name of Athens and instituted a common sacrifice, that of the Panathenaea."[85] The same boys and girls who had danced the *Geranos* in Delos thus returned to Athens with Theseus, who immediately gathered the Attic population and instituted the Panathenaea, a festival that centered upon a large piece of fabric: the peplos destined to cover Athena Polias on the Acropolis. We have sufficiently insisted on the political meaning of this ritual garment; here we would merely point out that the dance of the young Athenians of both sexes at Delos, weaving a metaphorical cloth (imitating another "fabric" that was never completed), prefigures the political weaving of Athena's peplos, which emphatically symbolizes the unity of all inhabitants of Attica.

Let us return to the *ekphrasis* of the *uestis* spread on the bed of Peleus and Thetis. Although Ariadne, to whom Catullus gives a voice for 70 lines,[86] is a being in the depths of despair, her story doesn't end on the shores of Dia. The poet relates what ensues, describing the arrival of Dionysus and his band of followers "in another part" of the tapestry.[87] On the margins of the scene, violently taken with Ariadne, the god approaches followed by Satyrs, Sileni, and maenads, the latter "raging with frenzied mind."[88] And it is here, with an evocation of the "barbarian" music of the Dionysian troop, that Catullus brings his long *ekphrasis* to an end.[89] Another nuptial fabric, the peplos of Dionysos, of which we have already spoken earlier, will soon cover Ariadne.

By comparison with the story accompanying the *ekphrasis*, that of the wedding of Peleus and Thetis is something of a poor relation, too static, in fact too happy to engage the poet's imagination; Catullus devotes only 38 lines to it,[90] adding on a long *cantus* performed by the Fates during the nuptial banquet.[91] The description of the wedding itself, however, contains certain noteworthy elements. The guests include not only Jupiter, the father of the gods, and his "divine wife" *(sancta coniunx)*,[92] but also the river god Peneus from the valley of Tempe. Like the others, he has brought wedding gifts—trees of various species. "All these he wove [*contexere*] far and wide around their home," says Catullus, "that the portal might be greenly embowered with soft foliage [*uestibulum . . . uelatum*]."[93] Thus, Peleus' home is itself as if enclosed within a weaving, a theme that the Fates will develop almost immediately in their own way: "No house has woven such loves as these [*nulla domus umquam tales contexit amores*]; no love ever joined [*coni-unxit*] lovers in such a bond."[94]

The "truthful song" of the Fates, who replace the Muses of the Pindaric scenario (in the third *Pythian Ode*),[95] is devoted to the hero who will be the fruit of the union of Peleus and Thetis, namely Achilles. Singing while spinning, the Fates already know as much about the hero as a Homer. They spin his destiny and sing it: "The left hand held the distaff clothed with soft wool; then the right hand lightly drawing out the threads with upturned fingers shaped them, then with downward thumb twirled the spindle poised with rounded whirl [*turbo*] . . . They then, as they struck the wool, sang with clear voice, and thus poured forth the Fates in divine chant. That chant no length of time shall prove untruthful."[96] After having addressed first Peleus, then the couple, the Fates recount the entire future of the son who will be conceived beneath the nuptial blanket,[97] finally returning to the couple, encouraging them to unite to their hearts' delight.[98]

On the bed of this joyous union lies the nuptial tapestry depicting an Ariadne abandoned by her husband. Union on the one hand, disunion on the other—a double, contradictory theme that, on a diachronic level, in terms of its outline of a history of humanity, will also be that of the conclusion of the Catullan *epullion*. For, says the poet, in the days of men like Peleus, the gods "were wont to visit pious homes of heroes, and show themselves to mortal company."[99] This blessed era irrevocably passed when "the earth was stained with hideous crime, and all men banished justice from their greedy souls":[100] fratricidal wars and incestuous relations have brought about a definitive separation of men and gods.[101] Union has given way to disunion.

Why did Catullus include the story of the unhappy wedding of Ariadne and Theseus within the story of the happy wedding of Peleus and Thetis? Why did he concentrate so much on the story that was subordinate (since it is included within the tale that occasions the story) that the misadventures of Ariadne and Theseus tend to surpass their own framework? Why this juxtaposition of two stories that are symmetrically balanced, just about equal in length, in a single poem? These are pertinent questions to which by way of response we propose another question: could it be that Catullus' text, in keeping with its subject, respects the principle of the union of opposites in its very conception, doing so in order to create a *textus*, which is to say a "fabric"? According to this hypothesis, the subject of the poem would in a sense have imposed the principle of weaving *(sumploke̅)* as its rhetorical model. (Didn't Hermogenes, the theoretician of rhetoric, demand that a discourse devoted to a flowery subject be composed in a "flowery" style?)[102] In other words, the poem, which interweaves the contrary but complementary themes of nuptial union and disunion, may itself be a "fabric," a metaphorical weaving, in short: a text.

It is true that the Latin word *textus* in the sense of "text" is not attested before Quintilian (who died in about 100). But the verb *texere*, "to weave," is already common in the sense of "composing a written work" in Cicero (106–43 B.C.), which makes our hypothesis perfectly admissible.[103] Like any other written work, a poem can be a "fabric"; this notion provides the poet with an easy response to the reproach of having written a poem containing contradictory elements: a *textus* is precisely that. If Catullus' text is to be understood as a fabric, might this poem not be the nuptial gift offered a couple celebrating their wedding? A metaphorical "nuptial fabric"? We believe in the possibility of such a metaphorical intention for the poem. After all, Plutarch dedicated his *Advice to Bride and Groom* to the couple Pollianus and Eurydice, whom he addressed in the preface of his work—it is the *logos* that is supposed to accompany the Hymenaeus heard by the couple in their nuptial chamber:[104] "I am sending it as a gift [*dōron*] for you both to possess in common; and at the same time I pray that the Muses may lend their presence and co-operation to Aphrodite."[105]

III

TEXTUS

5

THE CLOAK OF PHAEDRUS:
THE PREHISTORY OF THE
"TEXT" IN GREECE

AMONG the metaphors that have been used in the West—and elsewhere—to designate linguistic activity, weaving occupies a place of primary importance: the very etymology of the word "text" puts us on the trail of the history of this archaic metaphor, a history that could quickly grow to immense proportions given that other Indo-European languages besides Greek and Latin used similar ones.[1] It is indeed with a feeling of paradoxical familiarity that we tend to approach this ancient metaphorical universe, of which the "text" is but one surviving element—one that is relatively easy to reawaken from its existence as a linguistic fossil.[2] The aesthetic pleasure involved in rediscovering this metaphor and attempting to appropriate it for oneself is comparable to that of reactivating the meaning of other craft-related metaphors employed to designate well-constructed language or poetic creation. Rooted in a world in which the word and that which is "hand made," *Handwerk*, had a value they may have lost for us, the metaphor of verbal weaving seems to convey a distant truth, the lexical memory of which has been maintained by Indo-European languages. What could be more natural, under these conditions, than to imagine the author of the first great Western poems, the *Iliad* and the *Odyssey*, as a fabulous craftsman, able to "weave" his poems? This intuition is especially correct, it may seem, because the Greeks themselves chose the term *rhapsōidos*, "he who resews the song," to designate not the author, but the Panhellenic reciter of these same poems.[3] If the reciter can "resew the song," *rhaptein aoidēn*,[4] the song itself is necessarily a "fabric."

Unfortunately, this intuitive perception doesn't stand up to the facts. For the historical context in which the term *rhapsōidos* appears (as well as the related expression cited) is not that of the author of the Homeric songs. Thus it is impossible to know whether the *aoidē*, "song," was a metaphorical fabric for Homer. Moreover, in the two Homeric poems, both of which accord an important place both to the definition of their own status and to the description of weaving, there is not a single passage in which the author explicitly characterizes either his own song or that of a fellow bard as a "fabric."[5] Used in a comparable but considerably different manner, the metaphors of weaving and sewing are nonetheless known to Homer: Homeric gods and heros "weave" their clever tricks against an adversary; they "sew" his misfortune.[6] This "weaving" can also concern language itself.

In book 3 of the *Iliad*, the Trojan elders have assembled around Priam on the wall of Troy to witness the combat that will pit Paris against Menelaus, when suddenly Helen approaches. Upon the request of the king himself, the heroine identifies several Achaeans who can be seen before the city, first Agamemnon, then Odysseus. Antenor then begins to speak, recounting how one day the latter, accompanied by Menelaus, had come to Troy: "To both of these I gave in my halls kind entertainment, and I learned the natural way of both, and their close counsels [*mēdea pukna*] . . . Now before all when both of them wove their speech and their counsels [*muthous kai mēdea . . . huphainon*], Menelaus indeed spoke rapidly . . . But when Odysseus let the great voice go from his chest and the words came drifting down like the winter snows, then no other mortal man beside could stand up against him."[7]

Before the assembled Trojans, the two Greeks then begin to speak in order to convince the adversary of the opportuneness of a certain behavior on their part (no doubt the restitution of Helen). To succeed in their mission, they must carefully calculate the effect of their words, avoiding any spontaneous discourse: the possible desire for revenge they may harbor at this moment, for instance, must be kept under wraps. They must "control themselves." Their words are spoken with an objective strategy in mind, by which they hope to obtain their goal. From this perspective, it matters little whether their words are true or false: they appear—to Antenor, to Homer—as if manipulated or *handled* in the etymological sense of the word, the result of a manual operation, aiming to unite two opposites: the desire both to obtain Helen's restitution and to avoid wounding the Trojans' pride in the process—a desire that cannot be acknowledged without precaution, as it involves persuading the adversary that this restitution would be exactly what they should desire themselves. In their speech, the harshness of the request must in some sense unite with the gentleness of its rhetorical form. In other words, the request of the two Greeks must establish an equilibrium between two contradictory demands, opposed to each other like the warp and the woof in a tightly woven fabric. It must persuade without making any concessions. It must unite what is particular to the Greek position with what suits the Trojan position. Or, if one prefers, it must interlace one and the other. It is in this sense that Menelaus and Odysseus "weave" their *muthoi* and *mēdea*, their "words" and "counsels."

Thus Homer is familiar with the metaphor of verbal weaving. Yet he uses it to characterize not his own discourse, but rather the words spoken by the two kings before the adversary, in the midst of an assembly. Given that the author of the *Iliad* and the *Odyssey* had no lack of occasion, in the course of his long poems, to define these songs (or epic poetry in general) in terms of verbal weaving, it would be unwise to attribute the absence of "poetic weaving" to chance. Rather, this absence seems to have meaning; Homer may have had good reason not to "weave" his own songs. First of all, a bard does not consider himself to be the author of his own words. The Homeric poems make this quite clear: the words come to him from the Muse; she is the one who fills him with song. And this is true for the bards described in the poems as well as for Homer himself.[8] To claim to be able to "weave" a song would be a blasphemous act for them (regardless of whether the prohibition against "weaving" constituted a persisting religious belief

THE CRAFT OF ZEUS

or a constraint of the epic genre). The fate of Thamyris, recounted in the *Iliad*, is instructive in this respect, for it shows what happens to a bard who claims to sing better than the Muses and who thus contrasts his private words with those of the divinities of song: Thamyris is struck dumb.[9] In Homer's world, poetry is not private property.[10]

Second, the situation in which the two kings speak is distinguished clearly from that in which the Homeric bard sings the great deeds of heroes. The open setting of the assembly, where the interests of various parties are in opposition, is in contrast with the closed setting of the royal banquet, in which the bard's song aims to satisfy the demands of his listeners. The contradictory interests that characterize the assembly are in contrast to the bard's oneness with his listeners, a oneness in which he is guided by his Muse.[11] Whereas verbal "weaving" is in keeping with the context of the quasi-public gathering, characterized by the confrontation of opposing interests, it does not necessarily suit the bard's singing in the midst of a group with which he identifies—and must identify, in order not to jeopardize the automatic nature of his performance. To put it another way, whereas verbal "weaving" defines the receiver of the spoken words as an other, a stranger or a hostile party, the bard's song presupposes an identification between the sender and receiver that makes the metaphor unsuitable.

In order to compare his own art with that of a weaver, the bard must be more discreet. Barely 100 lines before the passage in which the two kings "weave" their words before the Trojan assembly, Homer recounts how the Greeks and Trojans prepare the combat between Paris and Menelaus, a combat that will put an end to the war and determine whether Helen will remain in Troy or return to Sparta. The goddess Iris brings the news to Helen, whom she finds "in the chamber; she was weaving [*huphaine*] a great web, a red folding robe, and working into it [*enepassen*] the numerous struggles of Trojans, breakers of horses, and bronze-armoured Achaeans, struggles that they endured for her sake at the hands of the war god."[12] Here, in the cloth she is weaving, the weaver depicts the same battles that Homer himself is in the process of telling. What does this inclusive procedure signify? If Homer were not so little inclined to define his song as a "fabric," it would not be an overinterpretation to say that the fabric was a metaphor for the song itself.[13] Things being what they are, however, we should draw no further conclusion from this juxtaposition of the poetic tale and the figured cloth than we would from the juxtaposition, for example, in Plato: "Thus," says Socrates in *Euthyphro*, "you admit that there truly are wars among the gods, terrible enmities, battles, and many such things, which poets relate, and which are represented to us by our good artists in various sacred ceremonies, for example at the Great Panathenaea, where we see the peplos to be carried to the Acropolis?"[14] The poems portray the same theomachies as the garments woven for the cult statues: but although the two types of representation are comparable, the fabric is no more the metaphor of the poem here than the poem is that of the fabric.

The connection between song and fabric need not be metaphorical in nature in order to be solid, as is shown by several passages in the *Odyssey* in which Calypso and Circe weave while singing. We will cite two of these. Arriving at Calypso's home, Hermes finds her "within . . . Indoors, and singing with sweet voice, she tended her loom and wove with golden shuttle."[15] A similar scenario occurs when Eurylochus and his men stop at the home of Circe: "They heard Circe singing in the house with sweet voice, while tending her great imperishable loom and weaving webs, fine, beautiful, and lustrous as are the works of gods."[16] As suggested by Jane McIntosh Snyder in her article "The Web of Song," this association between song and weaving in Homer was not insignificant for the lyric poets when they took the decisive step to represent song metaphorically as fabric.[17]

For ultimately, this step was taken. First in Pindar: "Weave [exhuphaine], sweet lyre, at once in Lydian melody this song [melos] also loved by the Vineland and Kypros," says the poet in the fourth Nemean Ode.[18] Thus the lyre is transformed into a loom, whose vertical warp corresponds to the vertical strings.[19] (Elsewhere the word mitos, "warp thread," is used in the sense of "lyre string.")[20] The poem becomes a musical fabric singing "in Lydian melody." In fact Pindar will make felicitous use of the semantic possibilities of the adjective "Lydian" later on. In the eighth Nemean, the poem becomes a "Lydian tiara," a mitra Ludia (an object known from the poems of Alcman and Sappho),[21] which is sonorously (kanachada) woven (pepoikilmena).[22] The Lydian melody, or key, of the victory ode thus suggests to the poet the metaphor of the Lydian tiara, designating the ode itself (as the scholiast confirms): "I bear a Lydian tiara, richly woven with music," he says to the victor, Deinias of Aegina.[23] A similar metaphor is found in a fragment: "I weave [huphainō] a tiara with rich designs [*poikilon andema*] for the Amythaonids."[24] In these two examples the poem is compared to a relatively small fabric—a bandeau, tiara, or diadem—rather than to a large piece of cloth. The reason for this is undoubtedly that the victory ode is supposed to *crown* the victor rather than cover him entirely; in any case, this particularity would not affect the fundamental meaning of the metaphor. On the other hand, the final example of Pindaric weaving does not specify the size of the fabric: "I drink of her splendid water [namely that of Theba]," says the poet in the sixth *Olympian Ode*, "weaving [*plekōn*] a hymn with rich designs [*poikilon humnon*] for fighting men."[25]

If this example leaves some doubt concerning the exact meaning of the verb *plekein*, which we translate as "to weave" (rather than "to braid"), basing ourselves on Plato and Theocritus (we could also invoke the meaning of *poikilon* here),[26] a first example taken from Bacchylides is not the slightest bit ambiguous in this respect. From his island of Ceos, the poet asks King Hieron of Syracuse to forget his troubles: "Turn your thoughts this way: with the help of the deep-girded Graces your guest-friend has woven a song of praise [*huphanas humnon*] and sends it from the sacred island to your distinguished city."[27] Whether this is an etymological figure or not,[28] Bacchylides considers that he "wove" his "hymn." Not that this metaphorical usage is dependent upon the written nature of the poem; on the contrary. It is interesting to note, however, that it is a poem that the poet "sends" *(pempei)* to his recipient:[29] the material and tangible nature of this epistolary ode in fact adds a new dimension to language weaving as we have studied it until now. In a poem addressed to the

Athenians, Bacchylides uses the same metaphor, calling on the "care for perfection" *(merimna)* characteristic of the poets from Ceos (his uncle Simonides and himself): "Weave [*huphaine*] something new in the rich beloved Athens, O famous perfectionism of Ceos!"[30]

Thus it seems that the choral poets, Pindar and Bacchylides, were the first in Greece to use the metaphor of weaving to designate poetic activity. They are thereby clearly distinguished from Homer, who never explicitly defined song as a fabric, although he was familiar with the metaphor of language weaving. What is behind this difference? While it may have had a certain importance for the poets who metaphorically represented their own song as fabric, the simple juxtaposition of weaving and song in Homer is not enough to explain this development, as J. McIntosh Snyder believes when she qualifies this juxtaposition as "fundamental"[31] (in any case the same "juxtaposition" existed in the daily practice of weavers, for song has always accompanied work). In our opinion, the reason for the change is to be found elsewhere.[32]

Unlike the Homeric bard, the choral poet composes his poems for public occasions, in which poetic praise will have the task of combatting the ill will of people who are jealous of the victor's success. A victory ode must forever assert the triumph of a contemporary who otherwise might be forgotten. Its author is a professional poet in the full sense of the word, receiving commissions from diverse clients who are often far away, as Hieron of Syracuse is from Bacchylides. In such a situation, the poet must assert himself as author of his poem, even if he has to invoke the Muse to ensure the "regularity" of his composition. For if

he doesn't assert himself as the author—the artisan, pro-
ducer, *poiētēs*—how can he ask that his client remunerate
him for his work? In other words, the poet who "weaves"
his poem finds himself in a situation that is entirely comparable to that of Menelaus and Odysseus. The poet's
interest in raising the price of the poem is at odds with that
of the client in keeping the price down, as we learn for
example in Aristotle.[33] Like Menelaus and Odysseus, the
poet is in a social situation in which the interest of one side
is opposed to that of the other. Like them, he must calculate
the effects of his words: if he agrees with what is said in
his poem, so much the better, but that's not what he's being
paid to do. His poem must simply obey the objective
strategy of praise: it must convince, even if its author isn't
convinced himself.

Under such conditions, the poem becomes the product
of a manual operation aiming to unite the skill *(sophia)* of
the poet and the raw material *(archa)* imposed by the
client[34]—or, if one prefers, aiming to interweave one and
the other. Poetic composition is a metaphorical weaving,
the result of which is a "richly patterned" fabric. Even
though this metaphor, once introduced in choral poetry, is
apt to produce a series of new meanings (for instance the
connotations of "Lydian" weaving in Pindar), the only way
to understand the contrast between the bard who doesn't
"weave" and the "weaving" of the choral poet is to compare their respective situations: one belongs to a closed,
unified world; the other, to an open and contradictory
world. The bard doesn't have to oppose his interests to that
of his listeners; he doesn't have to pose as the author of
his songs.[35] He is a member of the royal house, which is

neither an assembly nor a market. In contrast, the choral poet, working on contract for a growing number of clients, has no trouble asserting that he is the artisan of his odes, their "weaver."

If we have insisted on this contrast between Homer and the choral poets, emphasizing the novelty of the metaphor of poetic weaving in Pindar and Bacchylides, it is out of concern not to flatten out the history of the metaphor that interests us here: instead of reducing the difficult history of poetic weaving in Greece to a few lexical facts quickly integrated into the global Indo-European history of language weaving, we wanted to respect the fact that poetic weaving is resolutely absent from the Homeric poems and to try to understand why. The reductive tendency of the comparativist approach is inclined to erase the specific characteristics of a culture or of a cultural history in favor of an abstract synthesis, high in the Indo-European sky, where everything is "the same" because it must be.

If it is true that the invention of "poetic weaving" in the Greek language is due to choral poets—probably to Simonides, a pioneer in this domain (we could be more certain of this if our knowledge of his work were less fragmentary)[36]—the importance of their innovation can hardly be overestimated. Emancipating poetry from the religious universe to which it had belonged[37] (and to which it would long remain attached), the choral poets developed the basis for a reflection on language that greatly benefited the budding development of rhetoric and linguistics. Through metaphors that define discourse not only as something "woven" but also as a "construction," they insisted so much on the materiality of discourse that—in about

450 B.C.—they ended up being called *poiētai* ("artisans," "producers," "builders");[38] thus Homer himself could finally begin his career as a "poet."[39] It was at this time that the Sophist movement emerged, of which Simonides is cited as one of the secret prototypes by Plato:[40] theoreticians of language rather than poets, they would go further than their precursors, aided by the fact that the materiality of discourse had become literal, literate, scriptural.

Plato proves sensitive to this reflection on language when he too uses the metaphor of linguistic weaving: while disdaining the *poiētēs*,[41] the philosopher appropriates his metaphor in order to define the relationships between *grammata* united into syllables, in a context which we have already examined in detail. To introduce the paradigm of weaving in *The Statesman*, Plato uses the analogy of learning to read, the paradigm of paradigms.[42] How can children be taught to spell correctly syllables that they can't pronounce? The Stranger explains that one must juxtapose simple syllables and difficult ones so that the child can pick out similarities and differences in their respective *sumplokai*.[43] On the basis of a *sumplokē* of letters that are already known and considered easy, he will learn, by means of comparison, the way in which the *grammata* are "interwoven" into syllables that he doesn't yet know. The elementary operation of weaving, namely interlacing or *sumplokē*, is utilized here as a metaphor for the combination of letters into syllables. Vowels and consonants are "interlaced" or "woven together" to form syllables, some of which are already words, others of which will combine into words. It is thanks to a minimal "weaving" process on a phonological level that syllables and words are formed.

Thus this theory, *grammatik* in the proper sense of the word, concerns the most elementary level of language.

The metaphor of weaving recurs in another of Plato's dialogues, namely *The Sophist,* but this time on a syntactic level.[44] The Stranger points out to Theaetetus that the verbs "walk, run, sleep" do not form a discourse, a *logos.* Similarly, the nouns "lion, deer, horse" do not form a discourse either, for "the sounds uttered indicate neither action nor inaction nor being—either of a being or of a nonbeing—so long as one has not mixed some verbs with the nouns [*tōis onomasi ta rhēmata kerasēi*]." To obtain a discourse, one must combine the noun "lion" with the verb "walks," and so on: lion + walks, deer + runs, horse + sleeps. "Only then," continues the Stranger, "is harmony established [*harmozein*][45] and, instantly, the first *sumplokē* made into discourse, of all the discourses in some sense the first and the briefest." By "interlacing" *(sumplekon)* verbs and nouns, the *logos* "speaks" instead of just "naming." In reality, concludes the Stranger, *logos* is the harmonious union of two dissimilar things, of two contraries.

Thus, we see how the metaphor of weaving in its most elementary form, *sumplokē,* can play a role that is as important in the development of a grammar as it is in that of a political theory. Indeed, Plato gives us a glimpse of an entire linguistic theory based on the concept of *sumplokē,* a theory which he merely echoes and which may well have been far more important than these few passages of dialogue suggest. In fact it is not surprising that the author of *The Statesman,* half of which is devoted to political weaving, is so sensitive to theories based on linguistic weaving; we have also noted that he is equally attentive to the symbolism of the fabric signifying the union—in this case spiritual—of the couple lying beneath it: in the *Symposium* he depicts an Alcibiades lying with Socrates beneath the same *himation,* "cloak."[46] What may seem surprising is that we also find in Plato a theory of written communication arrayed in this same vestimentary symbolism.[47]

The point of departure of the *Phaedrus* is the reading of the discourse on the "beloved" written by Lysias. After hearing this discourse read by its author that very morning, Phaedrus is about to head outside the walls for a walk in the Attic countryside when he encounters Socrates. Phaedrus mentions Lysias' subject to the philosopher, who is anxious to hear the discourse: a summary of its contents will not suffice; he wants to hear the very words. At this, Phaedrus agrees to read it to him; he has the manuscript with him, as Socrates suspected. He settles beneath a plane tree and begins reading.[48]

Although this may seem a simple point of departure, in reality it is filled with meanings to which the interpretation of the dialogue as a whole must remain attentive, in order to avoid getting bogged down in the paradox of the written dialogue that condemns writing. What are these meanings? We will limit ourselves here to the essential one. Lysias is Phaedrus' lover. In their homoerotic relationship, Lysias is the active partner (the lover), Phaedrus the passive partner (the beloved). But here the lover is also the writer: Lysias wrote the discourse. Phaedrus will read this discourse out loud: the beloved here is thus also the reader. Now, within the Greek context, such a doubling of roles (the lover who doubles as a writer, the beloved who doubles as a reader) cannot be innocent: one of the first Greek models of written communication, in fact, defines the writer as a metaphorical lover, leaving the role of the beloved to the reader.[49] This "pederastic" metaphor stems in part from the fact that the Greeks of the first literate centuries read exclusively out loud: through his writing, the writer is supposed to use the reader, the indispensable instrument for the full realization of his written word. The writer uses the reader, just as the lover uses the beloved to satisfy his desire. It goes without saying that it is this relationship that Plato seeks to revolutionize in his dialogue, devoted both to *logos* and to *eros*.

The pertinence of these remarks for the interpretation of *Phaedrus* is confirmed by a passage in the beginning of the dialogue. Phaedrus is carrying Lysias' manuscript. Lysias is even considered to be "present" *(parōn)* because of this text:[50] the writer is present by the intermediary of his writing. And where exactly is this writing, which stands in place of the writer, to be found? Let us listen to Socrates addressing Phaedrus: "Very well, my dear fellow: but you must first show me what it is that you have in your left hand under your cloak; for I surmise that it is the actual discourse."[51] Lysias' discourse is found "under the cloak" of Phaedrus, *hupo tōi himatiōi*. Thanks to this discourse, Lysias is considered to be "present." The writer and the reader are thus covered by the same cloak. The nature of their relationship is symbolized by the fabric that covers them: "to go under the same cloak," as we know, meant nothing short of "sexually uniting" to the Greeks. The relationship between the writer and the reader is thus a sexual relationship, symbolized by the cloak—this real "text"—that covers them. Two Greek verbs seem to confirm this conclusion: *entunchanein* and *sungignesthai*, whose meanings overlap in the sense of "to read," also mean "to have sexual relations with."[52]

Thus a relationship is woven between the writer and the reader characterized by an opposition as distinct as that between the warp and the woof in the woven garment covering them. What does Phaedrus do that is so extraordinary that his relationship to Lysias should take this surprising form? He does not lie beneath his *himation* with Lysias in the same way that Alcibiades does with Socrates, but simply lends his voice to the voiceless writing. Phaedrus is necessary for Lysias' writing to be fully realized, for to the Greek mind, the writing by itself is incomplete. The addition of the voice is like a necessary "epilogue": the sound of the voice remedies the inanimate and silent nature of the writing.[53] Thus there is a distinct opposition between two absolute but complementary opposites: the warp here is the writing, which awaits only the woof of the reader's voice to be fully realized. This first "text"—the reader will allow us to use this term in the etymological sense—unites the writing and the voice in the act of reading, which means that it refers to a dynamic relationship rather than to a static object. Once the reading is over, its fabric will unravel into the written warp and the vocal woof—so that the warp can be used in other weavings, in other readings. The writing remains identical and stable, while the number of "texts" it makes possible is theoretically infinite.

Although Phaedrus' *himation*—the garment covering the writer and his reader—might not seem to allow for so precise an interpretation in and of itself, such an interpretation is nonetheless in conformity with the Greek experience of reading. For when reading out loud, what are "woven together" are not so much consonants and vowels, or nouns and verbs, but alphabetic signs and the voice of the reader, the meeting of which gives birth to what we have just, cautiously, referred to as the "text." What then happened when in certain circles the practice of reading silently began to take hold at the end of the sixth century B.C.?[54] The answer is not without consequence for our "text." For in the silent reading of the Greeks, the voice of the reader is in some sense transferred into the graphic sphere, which in turn raises *its* voice: the Greek who reads silently hears the "voice" of the writing in front of him in his head, as if the letters had a voice, as if the book were a talking object. In Euripides' *Hippolytus*, the writing is supposed to be capable of "speaking" to the reader who reads in silence, of "shouting" to him, even of "singing" him a *melos*.[55] It is as if the voice were inside the writing, present inside.

In other words, from now on writing and the voice seem to be lodged in the same place, and the "text"—created by the reader each time his voice unites with the writing—therefore becomes quasi-obsolete, replaced by a text that is closer to our own, which tends to erase the interpretative, or at least vocal, contribution of the reader (to such an extent that a considerable theoretical effort became necessary in the twentieth century to accord the reader an active role in reading). An unsuspecting ventriloquist, the reader now listens, in his head, to a text that seems to be addressing him autonomously. Naturally if he wishes to employ a more solemn, traditional process, he can read his text out loud. Reading then takes the form that a remarkable poem from the *Anthologia Palatina* depicts in allegorical fashion in an epigram attributed to Tiberius Ilus but which may date from the Hellenistic period: "Having woven his fine web with agile legs, a spider held a cicada prisoner in his treacherous toils. Seeing this dear friend of song groaning in its fine fetters, I was hardly indifferent upon passing near the spider, but undid the snare and freed the cicada, adding these words: 'Go free, you who sing with the voice of the Muses!'"[56]

As Democritus asserts, humans learned weaving from spiders.[57] The web woven by the spider is thus rightfully a *huphos* or a *textus*, two words signifying both "fabric" or "web" and "text."[58] Now, the spider in the epigram has woven a *lepton huphos*, a "fine web."[59] Have we the right to think that this weaving is metaphorical and that this "fine web" is also a "subtle text," the referent of which is the poem itself? We believe so, and for two reasons: (1) the status of the cicada in Greek thought, a status that leaves no doubt concerning the referent of the insect; (2) the logic of the poem, which is not a naturalistic study but an allegorical-type epigram not without parallel in the *Anthologia*.[60] What is the cicada's status? In Greek, cicada is pronounced *tettix*, a word that evidently seeks to imitate the sound of the insect.[61] The attention paid to the sound of the cicada is a good starting point, which one of Aesop's fables, "The Man and the Cicada," further clarifies.[62] To the man who caught it with the intention of eating it, the poor cicada cries for mercy, reminding its executioner that it is practically incorporeal; it is merely a voice, a *phōnē*. Indeed, the powerful sound of the cicada seems out of proportion to its body. For the Greeks, the song of the cicada was divinely beautiful, the most beautiful music imaginable.[63] Quasi-synonymous with voice, with a beautiful voice, the cicada symbolizes poetic voice in particular.[64] It is thus logical that this insect, a species of which is called *laketas*, is supposed to belong to Apollo—to "Sonorous" Apollo, *Lakeutēs*.[65]

Thus the cicada of the epigram is capable of signifying voice—the voice of the poet. And if this voice is trapped in a web, this web is inevitably the fabric of the poem itself, given that the metaphor of linguistic *sumplokē* as well as that of *huphos*, translating the Latin *textus*, is attested in Greek. The web of the poem is the arachnoid writing that holds the voice prisoner. But the poet seems to have foreseen this: he counts on the reader to read his poem and thereby to liberate the voice that this spider has so cruelly ensnared in the web it has woven. In other words, the poem constitutes the program for reading and thus for liberation. The reader "unties" the voice found within the very fabric of the poem, the voice caught in the threads with which the written poem is made. Each reader will thus liberate this "voice of the Muses" of which the poem speaks. An allegory of itself and of its own reading, this epigram thus opposes text and voice in a new fashion. "Subtly woven" by the spider, the web is no longer made of a written warp and a vocal woof as is the "text" we spotted in Plato. It is entirely scriptural.

In the "Greek prehistory" of the Latin *textus*, the spider's web whose meaning we have just identified actually constitutes a borderline case, or, if one prefers, a borderline text. There are two reasons for this. The first concerns the date: whether it belongs to the Hellenistic or to the imperial period, it is likely that this Greek poem was already under the influence of the Latin *textus*. Which is to say that its metaphor, or allegory, could already have been influenced by the success of *texere*—"to weave, to write"—in Latin. The second reason is situated on an entirely different plane: it has to do with the way in which the spider weaves its web. Even if the spider taught humans the art of weaving, it weaves by using only one type of thread, which it disposes with an "innate" sense of Euclidean geometry[66] but which nonetheless remains continuous and identical. Indeed, says Plutarch, one of the fundamental features of this admirable web is "the absence of a warp," *to mē stēmonōdēs*.[67] In the series of examples of language weaving that we have examined, the spider's text thus constitutes not only a kind of historical culmination but also, perhaps, a barely perceptible rupture with the *sumplokē* of opposites that is the feature common to all the examples of language weaving we have studied thus far. Although these opposites may be situated in various areas, they always figure within the logic of weaving understood as "the interlacing of the warp and the woof," the interlacing of one and the other.[68] Without a warp, the spider's web is distinguished from our series, the better to distinguish itself from the voice it holds captive.

6

THE BIRTH OF AN IDEOGRAM:
THE METAPHOR OF THE
TEXTUS IN LATIN

WHEREAS we conjectured in the preceding chapter that humans learned the art of weaving from the spider, a famous story from book 6 of Ovid's *Metamorphoses* seems to reverse this relationship, recounting the transformation of the weaver Arachne into a spider (*arachnē* in Greek).[1] For although the poet doesn't say so explicitly, it is quite likely the origin of spiders that is being written into fable (just as a similar legend told by Socrates in the *Phaedrus* retraces the origin of the cicada).[2] The contradiction is purely superficial, contrasting one tradition with another, for essentially in both cases what is targeted is the analogical—"mythical," we would say—link between human weaving and spider weaving. But the story of Arachne is also based on a well-known principle of Greco-Roman mythology (recall that the young weaver claimed to equal Minerva herself in the art of weaving).[3] Just as Thamyris—

who in the *Iliad* boasts of singing better than the Muses—is punished for his hubris (and forgets how to play the cithara in accompaniment),[4] Arachne too will be punished in her own way.[5] Yet her punishment is more reminiscent of that of the Pierides, to whose story a large part of book 5 of the *Metamorphoses* is devoted;[6] indeed, the Pierides' story immediately precedes that of Arachne, with which it is explicitly connected by Minerva at the start of book 6. This juxtaposition provides food for thought, for it places song and weaving side by side, as if the two were analogous phenomena.

Daughters of King Pieros, the nine sisters referred to as the Pierides present the Muses with a highly arrogant challenge: "Stop fooling the uneducated people with your sweet absurdities; if you have confidence in yourselves, goddesses of Thespiae, measure yourselves against us!"[7] With some hesitancy, the Muses take up this offensive challenge, and a jury of Nymphs is selected. One of the Pierides begins the competition. She sings a "reverse gigantomachy," according to which the Olympian gods are vanquished by giants and chased into Egypt, where henceforth they take on animal forms: Jupiter is transformed into a bull, Apollo into a raven, Bacchus into a goat, Diana into a cat, Juno into a cow, Venus into a fish, and Mercury into an ibis.[8] Next comes Calliope's song, which is naturally in keeping with the norms: the subject is the story of Ceres, the goddess of agriculture. It occupies practically half of book 5 and, as one would expect, wins the competition.[9] When, annoyed at their defeat, the Pierides continue their insults against the Muses, the latter transform them into magpies, a new species of bird that will henceforth fill the air with "raucous chatter" *(rauca garrulitas)*.[10]

This is a pleasant punishment for Minerva, who, at the very start of book 6, picks up the thread by saying: "Let us not allow our divinity to be so insolently slighted!"[11] Whereupon the weaving competition between the goddess and Arachne is recounted.[12] The daughter of humble parents—her father's name is Idmon, "know-how"[13]—Arachne became known throughout the cities of Lydia for her marvelous talent as a weaver: people came from all around to admire not only her completed works but also her technique—"so skillful was she at her work," says the poet.[14] Now, everyone assumed that Arachne was the student of Minerva, the goddess of weaving. "But she denied it, offended that people thought she'd been trained by a master, even a master so great. 'Let her do battle with me,' she said; 'if I'm defeated, I'll give in to anything.'"[15] Assuming the form of an old woman, Minerva visits Arachne to bring her to reason, yet manages only to provoke an even greater arrogance on the part of the girl, who asks, "Why is the goddess avoiding the competition?"[16] This is too much for Minerva, who resumes her form as a goddess. The Nymphs and the women present are terrified; only Arachne is unafraid. Everything is set for the competition.

Two looms are placed side by side. Minerva sets about representing a famous episode from the history of Athens, an episode opposing Neptune and herself (and which in fact was the subject of the western pediment of the Parthenon in Athens). The city would belong to the divinity who could prove that he or she would be the most useful, and thus Minerva, who with a blow of her lance brought an olive tree up from the ground, won. Around this central story, the goddess weaves four stories of hubris into the four corners of the cloth for the benefit of her human rival.[17] The latter chooses a series of images depicting the deceitful manner in which Jupiter, Neptune, Apollo, Bacchus, and Saturn united with mortal women, notably how Jupiter, transformed into a bull, stole Europe; how, metamorphosed into a swan, he united with Leda; how, in the form of a Satyr, he united with Antiope, the mother of Amphion and Zethos.[18] But the work is so well done that neither Minerva nor Envy personified finds the slightest fault with it. Furious, the goddess "tears up the colored fabric that reproduces the faults of the gods," striking Arachne on the forehead with her shuttle. Unable to bear the insult, the young weaver "ties a rope around her neck." At this point Minerva takes pity on her and grants her her life: "Live, miserable creature," she tells her, "but remain suspended in the air." Arachne is transformed into a spider. Yet, concludes Ovid, "she applies herself, as before, to her fabrics [*antiquas exercet aranea telas*]."[19]

The parallel between the song of the Pierid and the cloth woven by Arachne is only too clear: the lies of the one, insinuating that the Olympian gods were hunted down by giants, correspond to the insinuations of the other, depicting a series of adventures in which the Olympian gods, beginning with Jupiter, appear as systematically deceitful in their relationships with the mortals they desire. But the parallel doesn't stop there. As one might expect, it concerns the metamorphoses cast in song and in cloth by the two

contestants: even though each of the animal transforma-
tions obeys its own logic and diverges from the other in its
development, in fact both begin with the metamorphosis of
Jupiter into a bull, whether with the intention of humiliat-
ing him (as in the song of the Pierid)[20] or with that of
showing his dishonestly seductive nature (in Arachne's
fabric).[21] The presence in both stories of a metamorphosis
into a bull gives an indisputable indication of Ovid's intention: the juxtaposition does not occur by chance. Indeed it
seems to be an application of the famous formula of the
archaic Greek poet Simonides, already cited as a pioneer in
the area of poetic "fabrication": "Simonides . . . calls painting inarticulate poetry and poetry articulate painting."[22] In
Ovid, in retrospect, the song of the Pierid becomes a
weaving with a voice, while Arachne's weaving seems,
from the very start, a silent song. In other words, the
juxtaposition of the two stories seems to transform the song
into a metaphorical weaving and the weaving into a metaphorical song.

Now, such a metaphorical usage has already been suggested in book 3 of the *Iliad*, in which Helen weaves the
same combats that Homer is in the process of telling.[23] Yet
after an analysis of the implications that such an intention
would have for the bard, we ultimately decided against a
"metaphorical" interpretation of this passage. Basically, if
the metaphor of poetic weaving in its direct form ("I weave
a song") is notably absent in the Homeric poems, we feel
this absence is significant: for a bard to assert himself as
the "weaver" of his own songs would mean breaking his
ties to the Muse, who is the only one able to fill him with
song, as well as throwing into doubt the veracity of those

songs (the metaphor of language weaving being reserved for skillfully manipulable stories). For Ovid, who has all the "prehistory" of the *textus* behind him (and who, as we shall see, lives at a time when it is common to say that one "weaves" a written work), these considerations are obviously no longer valid, but it is nonetheless interesting to note that the song and the fabric in question are both false and blasphemous (whereas there is no parallel between the subjects of Calliope and Minerva). Contrary to what the Pierid asserts, the giants never overcame the Olympians. As for Arachne's weaving, humans simply have no right to insinuate or criticize a behavior that is "systematically deceitful" on the part of the gods. In a certain way, one could even say that the respective fates of the Pierid and Arachne are as eloquent as that of Thamyris in the *Iliad*, who is punished precisely because he contrasts his "own" song with that of the Muses, as if he, as a singer, possessed something that could be contrasted with the songs of the Muses, keepers of *all* song.[24]

With these reservations in mind, we are nonetheless convinced that the juxtaposition, in Ovid, of song and weaving tends metaphorically to render the song of the Pierid into fabric and Arachne's fabric into song. Clearly, this operation is not inconsequential for the status of Ovid's poem. As we suggested earlier in connection with Catullus' poem on the wedding of Peleus and Thetis, the poem itself seems to take on the status of a woven object. "Like spiders, we wove our intricate work," says the highly Ovidian author of the *Culex*,[25] with great frankness. The poem itself seems to assume the status of a *textus*, even though this word is found only in the century that follows. Like Ovid,

Catullus has the "prehistory" of this word behind him. It is impossible to imagine that he is not aware of the use of *texere* in the sense of "to compose a written work," a usage to which we have alluded and to which we shall return. In addition, he is perfectly aware of the great rupture that caused Homer's prudence in matters of poetic weaving to become superfluous, for his poem ends with a brief "history of humanity" whose turning point is the separation of men and gods.[26] Those who once lived together are now separate; if the divine and human worlds no longer communicate, the poet can no longer receive his words from the Muse. He no longer has anything to worry about in terms of poetic weaving; he can "weave his poem" if he likes. Simonides knew this, having been the first to emancipate poetry from its archaic religious universe.

Yet neither Catullus nor Ovid explicitly states that he "weaves" his poems. Why such discretion, comparable to Homer's monumental silence? This question cannot be answered in religious terms, as if our two poets feared committing an impiety. It does seem possible, however, to respond to it on another level, that of style; in particular, it is worth quoting from Longinus, who in his treatise *On the Sublime* writes: "The best rhetorical figure seems to be one that hides the very fact that it is one."[27] It would not be farfetched to imagine that this would have been Catullus' or Ovid's position: the obvious figure is to be avoided. If the operation by which the poem is metaphorically rendered into a fabric is not discreet, the metaphor is badly used; a lesson to which the author of the pseudo-Virgilian *Ciris* remained singularly blind—fortunately for us, we might add, for it is in its long preamble (lines 1–100) that the metaphor of the poem as a fabric is finally stressed as adamantly as one could wish.[28]

The title of the poem is the name of a bird, in Greek a *keiris*, into which its protagonist, the daughter of King Nisos of Megara, will be transformed. This king had an extraordinary head of white hair with one streak of red or purple on which his kingdom and his life depended. Now, when King Minos placed Megara under siege, the princess, Scylla, fell in love with him and decided to cut off[29] her father's magic lock of hair. Megara fell into the hands of Minos, who, without pity for the princess (whom the poem nonetheless calls his *coniunx*),[30] drags her in the wake of his ship before she is finally turned into a bird.[31] This, strictly speaking, is the content of the poem (lines 101–541). Its ties to poetic "weaving" seem rather artificial: in the preamble, the poet apologizes for the limited scope of the metamorphosis he is about to recount, adding that the Scylla in question is not the one who appears in the *Odyssey*. In the manner of a Callimachus or a Propertius, he merely defends his right to compose on "minor" subjects—especially since he is at the start of his career[32]—while promising Messalla, for whom the poem is destined, that he will later devote himself to more important subjects.

But perhaps the metaphor employed in the preamble and the metamorphoses of Scylla are not as unconnected as all that. For the Greek name of the bird after which the poem is named, *keiris*, is glossed by Hesychius with the word *alkuon*.[33] In other words, Scylla was transformed into a halcyon, that is, a kingfisher, the bird that Alcman qualifies as *hali-porphuros*,[34] alluding to its two main colors, ultramarine and purple. Might this purple be in memory of the lock cut from the head of Nisos? Whatever the case may be, the halcyon, the male of which is called *kerulos*[35] (Aristophanes is familiar with the neighboring form *keirulos*,[36] which is even closer to *keiris*), is doubly associated with weaving. First of all, metaphorically the halcyon designates the Greek weaver's shuttle, according to an epigram in the *Anthologia Palatina*.[37] "Shuttle," moreover, is *kerkis* in Greek, a word that is a paronym of *keiris;* and we might also note the common expression *kerkis aoidos*, "singing or twittering shuttle,"[38] which seems to fit within the same *concetto*. Thus the shuttle *(kerkis)* sings like a bird, or a halcyon *(keiris)*. Second, the halcyon is supposed to "weave" *(huphainein)* its nest: Aelian is emphatic on this subject.[39] The halcyon is thus a "weaver." This relationship, in our opinion, suggests that the *Ciris* is based on a Hellenistic poem, the implications of which the young Latin poet was unable to render in his adaptation. For what could be more natural than to introduce the metaphor of poetic weaving into a poem whose title may be understood as "The Shuttle-Bird" or "The Weaver-Bird"? Did our young pseudo-Virgilian poet understand this? Or did he merely adopt elements of an incompletely understood Greek original, in which the metaphor of poetic weaving was associated with the *keiris?*

In any case, it is now time to examine this metaphor more closely. The poet of the *Ciris* begins his preamble by asserting that he would like to devote a poem to an elevated, philosophical subject but that he doesn't want to "prohibit himself from weaving to the end [*detexere*, perhaps translating *exhuphainein*] the work he has begun [*coeptum . . . munus*]."[40] The first instance of the metaphor of poetic weaving thus concerns the *Ciris* itself, which the poet is determined to "weave to the end." He continues, repeating to Messalla that he would be only too ready to devote himself to a philosophical poem "if, right now, Science were to plant me on the summit of its acropolis":[41] the acropolis *(arx)* is that of Athens, and Science *(Sapientia)* is Greek philosophy. From such an elevated position, the poet could look at the world from above and wouldn't have to offer his patron such a simple poem as the *Ciris* (although, he adds, it is pleasant to amuse oneself in poetry from time to time).[42] In reality, he would like to offer him an entirely different sort of poem.

What he would like, in effect, is to "weave" the name Messalla "into a great peplos, if I may speak in this way [*magno intexens, si fas est dicere, peplo*]"[43]—a peplos "such as one brings to Minerva in Athens, the city of Erechtheus, to pay homage to her."[44] Is it proper to speak in this way? Not for a Homer—and we have explained why—but certainly for a Roman poet in the era of Augustus. The struggles of Minerva "are woven" *(texuntur)* into this peplos in fact:[45] the same gigantomachy that was mocked by the Pierid of the *Metamorphoses* is thus restored to its traditional meaning. "Such is the veil [*uelum*] that they bring every four years to the goddess," says the poet, referring to Minerva's peplos, mounted as a sail on the mast of a ship on wheels, and which we mentioned in the first chapter. And he continues: "Similarly, I would like to weave you [*intexere*, perhaps translating *enhuphainein*][46]—among the red suns and the white stars of the moon whose celestial chariot rocks the sky—into a magnificent poem devoted to the nature of things [*naturae rerum*], so that our page will bear your name, linked eternally to science by my song for men to come."[47]

Decidedly, nothing is missing from this poetic weaving, which specifies precisely of what the intercrossing or interlacing—the Greek *sumplokē*—consists: as in Pindar, the poet's expertise will combine with the subject matter, imposed by the person for whom the poem is destined, into an "eternal"[48] fabric. And as if this weren't enough, the preamble ends with an appeal to the Muses themselves, whom the poet asks to "weave" a border of eternal glory for his new book *(nouum aeterno praetexite honore uolumen)*,[49] as if it were a *praetextae*.

As we know, the author of the *Ciris* is not being innovative, either with respect to the Greek tradition, to which he proves only too faithful—his metaphor of poetic weaving descends directly from the idiom developed by the Greek choral poets—or with respect to his own language, in which *texere* had become common in the sense of "to compose a written work, to write" during the Ciceronian era. As we have mentioned, a Catullus could rely on his readers to have an strong familiarity with the metaphor of the *textus*. Let us therefore review a number of Ciceronian passages to examine the state of this metaphor. Our first example is taken from *Letters to His Friends:* "What do you think of my letters? Is not the style I use to write to you entirely vulgar? One cannot always write the same way. What do a letter, an address given before the court, or a public speech have in common? Besides, not all my court speeches follow a single model. I plead the private cases, those that aren't very important, with greater simplicity; the affairs that have life and reputation at stake, on the contrary, in a more elaborate style. As for letters, I usually weave them with everyday words [*quotidianis uerbis texere*]."[50] We have quoted this passage at length in order to highlight the lack of stylistic effort involved in Cicero's use of the word *texere*. Not only does he say that he "weaves" his letters with phrases from everyday life, but he also employs the metaphor of weaving as if it were an entirely common usage.

Which doesn't mean that from a stylistic point of view the Ciceronian *texere* applies exclusively to an epistolographic level of writing. In another letter Cicero speaks of a philosophical work in nine volumes that he has begun and rewritten several times: "I had divided the interview into nine days and as many books, the subject of which were the best type of political constitution and the ideal citizen; the work was weaving wonderfully [*sane texebatur opus*], and the dignity of the personages added great weight [*aliquantum . . . ponderis*] to the words I was attributing to them."[51] Three observations are in order regarding this passage. First, we see here that scriptural "weaving" applies not only to the writing of an ordinary letter but also to the composition of a dialogue devoted to an elevated subject. Next, the subject at hand is the best constitution: it is impossible here not to think of Plato's *Statesman*, a work dominated by the metaphor of political weaving, which may well have suggested to Cicero the use of the metaphor of "woven" composition. Finally, the "weight" of the interlocutors' discourse is considered to be proportional to their dignity: this notion suggests an amusing development with respect to the metaphor of fabric, since its quality depended on the weights (in Greek, *laiai*) that held the warp stretched.[52]

In addition to the epistolary and philosophical uses of the metaphor of scriptural weaving, a third type appears: speaking of the composition of historical works in the *Laws*, Cicero emphasizes that a great deal of time is required both for their preparation and for their composition. To which he adds the following: "It usually disturbs my train of thought, when I have once begun [*orsus*] a task, if I am forced to turn my attention elsewhere; nor do I find it as easy to take up the weaving [*contexo*] of an interrupted task as I do to complete at once whatever I have undertaken."[53] As in the preceding citation, we note a development of the metaphor of scriptural weaving: *ordiri*, "to mount the warp of a fabric, to warp, to begin" (of which *orsus* is a participial form), falls into the same metaphorical universe as *texere*—of which *contexere* is a compound form, the prefix of which refers to the fact that the weaving was interrupted and that it is necessary to begin with what has already been woven.

The same compound verb is found in our final example from Cicero: "Here I may repeat what an eminent man, Marcus Crassus, deploring the arrival of King Ptolemy, said not long ago: 'Would that in the woods of Pelion (the ship) had not . . .' And indeed I could pursue this poem by weaving [*ac longius quidem mihi contexere hoc carmen liceret*]: 'For never my wandering mistress' would have caused us this trouble, 'Medea sick at heart, wounded by cruel love.'"[54] As in the preceding example, the prefix *con-* refers to the idea of picking up with a given fabric that is

incomplete or mutilated, and its completion. More important, the use of the metaphor brings to light the fact that
the Ciceronian *texere* applies not only to the composition
of letters, philosophical dialogues, or historical works but
also to poetic composition (of which Cicero had practical
knowledge, since he had written a poem in hexameters on
his consulship, in addition to translating Aratus into Latin).
For the citations that follow one another in the quoted
passage are metrical: we are dealing here with poetry.

How are we to understand the *naturalezza* with which
Cicero employs the scriptural or poetic *texere?* What opposites does he unite in his writings by a metaphorical weaving? The opposition comes to mind, of course, between a
given character participating in philosophical dialogue and
the discourse Cicero attributes to him: if the dialogue "is
woven," it is undoubtedly, in part, precisely because of the
necessity of interweaving what is objectively given—since
the characters in the dialogue are all historical—and the
philosophical project. But this may not be the most important element.

Cicero was a key figure in the great process of acculturation by which Rome appropriated Greek culture.[55] Thanks
to him (and to many others), Greek thought found Latin
words to express itself anew. In other words, we are suggesting that it was the triumphant acculturation of the
Romans that partly explains the encroachment of the metaphor of linguistic and poetic weaving from Cicero's period
on (if not earlier). For the metaphor of weaving becomes
especially pertinent to someone who is engaged in trans-
posing an entire culture into a new milieu. Before becoming
worn out and common, the metaphor is likely to invade

(even to obsess) the mind of a man who undertakes this interweaving of opposites. And this situation is no less marked in the domain of poetry. All Latin poetry—with the exception, perhaps, of satire—obeys the logic of this growing acculturation.[56] When Catullus writes his poem on the wedding of Peleus and Thetis, his "weaving" has meaning connected to the occasion of the poem and the symbolism of the nuptial fabric, of course, but inevitably the poem-fabric also becomes a fabric on an "intercultural" level. It is a place where two cultures meet. And here, it is as if Catullus were using a Greek warp—the traditional basis for his poem—into which he introduces his own Latin woof, as if the best text were made of a Greek warp and a woof of Latin words.

The reader will certainly have noticed that in Cicero's first three citations, the "weaving" in question is a scriptural one. In Rome, it is mainly by writing that one "weaves." This is different from the situation in Greece, where, as we have noted, language weaving does not exclusively signify writing. In one of his *Victory Odes* cited earlier, the poem sent from his native Ceos to King Hieron in Sicily, Bacchylides barely suggests the written nature of his "weaving."[57] In Greece, it is certainly not the writing that makes the "weaver," whereas in Rome, language weaving is constantly—though not exclusively—associated with writing, as if it were perceived differently by the Romans. In our opinion, this difference is based on the history of writing within the two cultures—or, more exactly, on the specific moment when alphabetical writing appeared in each one.

For the Greeks, an entire series of major developments had already occurred on the level of mentalities when writing began to play a determining role. For the Romans, on the contrary, cultural development would be determined by writing practically from the start. The difference between the Greek *nomos* and the Latin *lex* is in this respect highly instructive: in keeping with its etymology, the Greek word can designate a law pronounced orally without the intervention—even prior intervention—of writing as well as a law read out loud, while the Latin word, which also means "law," fundamentally signifies "reading," thus *presupposing* the writing.[58] This significant difference suggests, in our view, that the development of language weaving in Latin occurred in the context of the constant presence of the written word.

Of course this written word could be inscribed on a palm leaf, tree bark, lead cylinder, fabric, or wax-coated tablet, as Pliny the Elder says in book 13 of his *Natural History*.[59] But the most important medium for alphabetical writing was undoubtedly papyrus, to which the same author devotes some remarkable pages in his book. His reason is simple: "The use of paper is essential for the development of civilization, in any case to record its memories."[60] Papyrus, he explains, comes from Egypt; and although Varro says it was unknown before Alexander, Pliny knew that the philosophical treatises of King Numa were written on papyrus, which was conserved for more than half a millennium inside the royal sarcophagus.[61]

The plant was used in several ways that were unrelated to writing: it was used for heating and for the production of domestic utensils; the Egyptians used it to "weave" *(texunt)* boats, sails, matting, clothing, mattresses, and ropes; the stump could be chewed.[62] "To make paper

THE CRAFT OF ZEUS

[*charta*],[63] one uses a needle to separate the fibers of the papyrus into strips that are as thin and broad as possible."[64] Next Pliny explains the relationship between the origins, within the plant, of these strips and the different qualities of paper obtained. Then he continues: "All papyrus is woven [*texitur*] on a table moistened with Nile water, the silt of which has the effect of a glue. The strips are first spread lengthwise; those that are too long on each end are trimmed, and another layer of strips is laid across on top. They all go together under a press, the sheets are laid in the sun to dry, and are then joined together according to their quality."[65] Finally, Pliny discusses the format and quality of the different types of paper.

The fineness of "Augustan paper," he explains, presented disadvantages that the Emperor Claudius wished to remedy: "Beginning with Claudius, the warp [*statumina*] was made with lesser quality [thus, less fine] strips and the woof [*subtemina*] with those of first quality."[66] For a Roman (and indeed for us), the resemblance between a true fabric and papyrus is striking—to the point that Pliny continues the image of weaving down to the details. The analogy has its obvious limits: the "weaving" of the papyrus *poses* the woof over the warp, without interlacing, and *glues* them together. But this technical difference apparently presents no problems for the analogical mind, and the fact that the same Romans who developed the metaphor of language weaving were in constant contact with this "woven" papyrus undoubtedly produced a scriptural orientation in their use of the metaphor. In fact Cicero "wove" his works precisely on this writing material: Pliny claims to have seen papyri written by the hand of the great Latin author.[67]

The same scriptural orientation of the metaphor of fabric, or of the metaphor of weaving, characterizes a usage already discussed in the chapter devoted, among other things, to Roman *peplophoria* (a usage that is especially important because it preceded Cicero's by a good generation). Recall that the first document to which we alluded was the Sibyl's oracle reported by Phlegon of Tralles. Let us now reread the beginning of this document: "In Rome, an androgyne was also born . . . For this reason, the Senate asked the decemvirs to consult the Sibyl's oracles. The decemvirs performed an exegesis[68] of the oracles, the content of which was as follows: 'The fate of mortals, who discover their individual paths only after the fact, what omens and what sufferings divine Destiny prepares for them, will be revealed by my *histos* [loom or fabric].'"[69]

Thus in Rome we have a document written in Greek and dating from 125 B.C.: the Sibyl's oracle, which refers to itself by the word *histos*, "fabric." Whereas acculturation normally takes the form whose implications we attempted to understand earlier, namely that of a Latin translation of Greek realities, the Sibyl's oracle is written in Greek—in "decemvir's Greek," leaving much to be desired on a grammatical level. It therefore constitutes an inversion with respect to the model that would become common, translating Roman realities into Greek—in Rome. A situation apt to perplex the Hellenist and Latinist alike.

What is a Sibylline oracle? One may recall the deal concluded between the Sibyl and King Tarquin, who ended up buying three books from the venerable Cumaean. These three books were deposited in the temple of Capitoline Jupiter, where they remained until they were destroyed by a fire that ravaged the temple in 83 B.C. An attempt was then made to reconstruct them by gathering together copies that existed in Italy and in Asia Minor. To distinguish the true oracles from fakes, one checked to see whether they were written in acrostics or not, acrostics constituting the only reliable criteria for authenticity.[70] Now, in the oracle dating from 125 B.C., whose beginning we have just read, this acrostic principle is respected. The first verse of the oracle is repeated as a "vertical border" on the left side of the first oracle (the second oracle obeys the same principle). In other words, the letters of the first verse are used, in the order in which they appear, as the first letters of the verses that follow. A first hexameter of forty letters would thus give a text of forty lines. If the oracle is a fabric, the acrostic constitutes its *pretext*, in both senses of the word.[71]

And this "fabric" or *histos* is not, as Cicero emphasizes, the product of an inspired "madness," but on the contrary the result of erudite work.[72] How did the decemvirs' consultation of the Sibylline books function? This is a difficult question, to which we propose a synthetic response in order to avoid entering into the details of a demonstration. Upon the Senate's request, the decemvirs responsible for the Sibylline oracles went to the place where the books were stored. In one way or another, one or several verses were selected—perhaps by lot?—and on the basis of this or these verses the construction of the oracle, its "weaving," began. This procedure would explain the pertinence, with respect to the context, of the oracles cited by Phlegon.[73] Thus the decemvirs' exegesis consists in selecting the verses to be used and in "weaving" the oracle to be presented to the Senate.[74] By becoming a crossword constructor and hexametric poet, the person who performs the exegesis respects both the Sibylline tradition and the crisis situation to which the oracle must provide an adequate response. For the Sibyl, without a doubt, has a hand in things; by the verses selected from her books she guides the composition of the oracle, whose hexameters, though often erroneous from a formal perspective, are never wrong concerning the basics: prescribing rites that, before any consultation of the Sibylline books, the decemvirs know only too well.

The "weaving" of the Sibyl and of the Ten Weavers thus turns out to have a very precise technical implication: it signifies the union between the hexameter selected, which is fixed and inalterable, and the sequence of verses that will be generated from it in light of a crisis situation. It signifies the interlacing of the traditional "hard" statement and its malleable exegesis, which is attentive to the present. But generally this fabric or *histos* also possesses another significance: made up of Greek words, it prescribes rites that will be accomplished "Greek-style" *(Achaisti)*[75] by Romans, in Rome. It is the meeting of two cultures, a place of intersection, a place where opposing realities interlace.

Thus the metaphor of language weaving is at the center of a series of oppositions: of the poet's expertise with the imposed subject matter, of the Latin language with the Greek reality, of the Roman reality with the Greek language; it opposes a philosophical project with the historical personages that are its voices (in the Ciceronian dialogue); the demands of the present with the fixed word of tradition. And all this against a very precise background: papyrus, which in itself opposes a woof of horizontal fibers with a warp of vertical ones. The only major absence from this

THE CRAFT OF ZEUS

list is the opposition between the *scriptural warp* and the *vocal woof*—an opposition which we believe we detected in Plato's *Phaedrus* and which is peculiar to oral reading, in which the "text" is the ever-unique encounter between the written word and the voice.[76] This absence is all the more surprising because reading out loud was the most common form of reading both in Rome and in Greece, as an epigram from the *Anthologia Latina* demonstrates: "When you read, I am speaking, for your voice is mine."[77] This defines the "model of vocal appropriation" that dominated all reading in antiquity. Does it imply that the absence to which we are alluding is absolute? Of course not.

"When you possess long-since published books of which you approve, O reader, and which are capable of giving pleasure through the quality of their style, why do you weave anew [*retexis*] the page [*paginam*] of our little book—so full of bagatelles and frivolities—which I, a mere beginner, have written in a youthful spirit to amuse myself? But what if this little work is dear to the learned thanks to its verses, though resounding with poor rhetoric and lacking in beauty and impressive phrasing? In that case you are right in asking for it and in starting to read it of your own will, as if you were watching a play on the stage!"[78] This is the complete text of a little Latin poem included in the book of epigrams published by Luxurius in 520 or 530 in Carthage, in the North Africa of the Vandals, under the reign of Hilderic or of Gelimer.[79] There are two reasons why we have chosen to conclude with a text of such a late date: first, because like "The Spider and the Cicada" in the Greek domain,[80] this work constitutes a *borderline text*, which it seemed to us would be appropriate near the end

THE BIRTH OF AN IDEOGRAM   151

of our final chapter; and second, because it alludes to a problematic peculiar to reading in ancient times, opposing the writing with the reading voice.

The allusion is subtle, it is true: for it all turns upon a single word that has long disturbed commentators on this poem, many of whom have wished to replace it, against the manuscript tradition.[81] This word, as one might expect, is *retexis*, "you reweave," in a place where, as Hans Happ observes, one would expect a word meaning "you read."[82] If the "rewoven" page is a silent column that the reader, in keeping with the usual practice, reads out loud, it follows that writing constitutes the warp of a fabric into which the reader inserts his own vocal woof. In other words, reading, not the written object, constitutes the "text," unifying the dead letter and the living voice, in a manner reminiscent of the *Phaedrus*, in which the writing of the absent Lysias unites with the reader, Phaedrus, in order fully to realize itself. Writing needs the reading voice in order to realize itself as a "fabric": this, in our opinion, is the myth that renders the use of the verb *retexere* intelligible in Luxurius. The writing is a warp into which the successive readers of the poem—beginning with the author—introduce their own woofs, each reading constituting a unique acoustic text, unraveled by silence only to be "rewoven" with each new manifestation in sound. Implicit in the metaphor used by Luxurius is a dynamic theory of the text, which is meant to consist not of an object but of an encounter between the writer and the reader in the reading.

Thus we have arrived at the end of our journey. One might wonder what became of the key word in all this, namely *textus*. The truth is that in this story of language weaving, largely centered upon the verb *texere,* the first attestation of the noun *textus,* in the first century of our era, becomes a simple formality. For in our opinion there is no reason to attribute particular importance to the fact that the *noun* did not appear earlier: it may well be a fluke, for it seems difficult to imagine any reason why a Cicero would have been prevented from using a substantive based on the verb *texere,* "to weave, to write." But in any case it is in Quintilian, a professor of rhetoric like Luxurius, that *textus* and *textum,* so familiar to us, appear for the first time. "If there is a kind of secret power in musical rhythms and modes, it is very alive in discourse: just as the value of a thought varies according to the words that express it, so that of words varies according to the arrangement that joins them, whether in the fabric [*in textu*] or at the end of complete sentences, for there are sentences in which the thoughts are poor and the expression mediocre and in which this is the only merit."[83] The value of words thus varies according to their place in the "fabric" of the phrase (or in the cadence of the sentence): as far as the metaphor of language weaving goes, Quintilian is not being innovative in this passage, for we know, for instance, that Plato had already thought of syntax in terms of weaving. On the other hand, another passage is remarkable in its "material" implications: "Perhaps they followed a different system from Demosthenes or from Plato, who were different from one another besides. For in Lysias, the fine and polished stylistic fabric [*illud in Lysia dicendi textum tenue atque rasum*] was unspoiled by excessively rich rhythms, which would have caused it to lose the grace—so remarkable in his work—of its simple, unadorned color, and would have caused it to lose merit as well."[84] Here the metaphor of the stylistic "fabric" leans visibly on the "fabric" constituted by the papyrus, of which Pliny, as we have noted, described the "fineness" and the preparation by polishing.

At about the same time that Quintilian was writing *Institutio Oratoria*, from which our two quotations are taken, Longinus wrote his famous treatise *On the Sublime*,[85] a work of capital importance that in a central passage uses a word corresponding to the Latin *textus*: "One or two passages are not enough to show the skill of the invention, the order and the disposition of the material; we barely see these qualities through the fabric [*huphos*] of the work; but when the sublime [*hupsos*] explodes where it should, it's like lightning: it disperses everything in its way, revealing the concentrated forces of the orator."[86] Thus Longinus opposes the lightning of the sublime, capable of dispersing everything in its way, with the patiently woven "fabric." His sympathies fall decidedly on the side of the "lightning" rather than that of *huphantikē*, but he seems nonetheless to be one of the first to have used the Greek word *huphos* in a "modern" sense, comparable to Quintilian's use of *textus (textum)*. It is very likely that this is a *Greek translation* of a Latin concept. For Longinus also lived under the empire of the Roman *textus*.

Now, if we compare these two words, *textus* and *huphos*, one difference literally jumps out at us, a difference likely to explain the subsequent destiny of the former, as well as that of the Ciceronian *texere*: the presence of the letter *x* in the middle of the word. Are we serious in asserting this? Absolutely. The truth is that no letter more precisely suggests the myth of weaving better than the *x*, the crossing of opposing threads. In other words, we are suggesting that the fascination right up to the modern period with the word *textus,* in its various forms, can be attributed to its *ideo-grammatic nature.* Not that we wish to critique the sign's arbitrariness here—far from it. As enlightened Cratylists,[87] however, we would simply like to emphasize that the arbi-trary sign is apt to become infused and invested, "after the fact," with significant values[88]—which sometimes give us the impression that the divine Namer "foresaw everything." Indeed, it is as if he had understood that, given its spelling, the word *textus* was the best designation for the thing designated. This is not the case for *huphos,* which is merely an obedient translation of the metaphor of *textus,* unable to produce the graphically distinctive sign of the Latin word, and which in fact has not preserved the meaning of "text" in modern Greek. This may be a kind of lexical Darwinism which we will cautiously avoid claiming to be widespread, but which may well explain the success of a word that in its long history has been able to suggest, almost imperceptibly, its deepest meaning, its myth, through the letter found in the center of its body.

Appendix A

NOTE ON
BIOLOGICAL "TISSUE"

FOR WHOEVER wishes to retrace the prehistory of the concept of histology—a word of fairly recent fabrication—or, more modestly, to find the origin of an expression such as "body tissues," a verse from the Psalms seems to furnish a solid point of departure: "For it was you who formed my inward parts; you wove me together in my mother's womb," sings David.[1] For the psalmist, the formation of the fetus constitutes a metaphorical weaving.

We find nothing of this sort in the Greco-Roman domain; for although the Greek atomists consider that everything is conceived or engendered by *sumplokē*, by interlacing, even by weaving,[2] the metaphor of corporeal weaving doesn't appear in Greece or Rome with the same simplicity as in the Psalms. With regard to the notion of procreation, the explanation seems obvious: in our discussion of the wedding of Peleus and Thetis in Chapter 4, we saw that the conception of Achilles was placed under the sign not of weaving but of *spinning*. It is true that the spinning of the Fates or Parcae, corresponding to the Greek Moirai, falls into the category of "wool work," but the intervention of the three goddesses does not take the form of weaving in Catullus' poem.

Singing the hero's destiny, the Fates dexterously produce the "thread" of his life. In the poem this "thread" is called *subtegmen*,[3] designating, as we know, the woof thread that the weaver will introduce horizontally into the vertical warp of the loom. Speaking specifically of Achilles' destiny, Horace will also have recourse to this term: the Fates "broke the hero's return" by a "firm woof thread," *certo subtemine*.[4] A curious statement at the very least, whose meaning is not immediately apparent. For it is not, as one might think, the *subtemen* that is broken: rather this is the *means* by which Achilles' return is canceled. It is not in the nature of the *subtemen* to be suddenly broken; it is the *stamen*, the "warp thread," that undergoes this operation— when the fabric is completed.

Elsewhere, we learn that it is the *stamina* that are "broken" by the Fates, as in the funerary hexameter "Suddenly the Fates broke the white thread of your destiny [*stamina*; literally: your white warp threads]."[5] If the *stamina* constitute the thread of Achilles' destiny, then this is the thread that is cut before his return to his native land. It will be symbolically crossed or "interrupted" by the fatal woof thread, the final *subtemen*, characterized as "firm" by Horace (just as the fateful day is "firm"). Thus the *stamen* is the vertical "thread of destiny," which in the course of the individual's life will be traversed by a multitude of *subteg-*

mina, "warp threads," until the last one, symbolizing the fatal event—like the arrow that would kill Achilles[6]—crosses the final *stamen*.

Thus in the Roman imagination life takes the form of a weaving, in which the woof thread ("the thread of destiny"), spun for each individual upon his conception or birth, will limit the course of his life. Conversely, the warp thread symbolizes the events in which the individual will become involved.

Now this "weaving" of the life of an individual is encountered not only among the Romans but also among the Greeks. Richard Onians, who devoted several remarkable pages to the "weaving of destiny" in the Greco-Roman world, quotes an anonymous lyric fragment in which the Moirai are asked to "weave [*huphainein*] with iron shuttles."[7] What would this thread be for if not for weaving? Nonetheless, the fact remains that it is not weaving but *spinning*—by Klotho, one of the Moirai (whose name is derived from the Greek verb *klothein*, "to spin")—that is in the foreground when Greeks and Romans think of the destiny of an individual. It is as if the fabric represented only the *finished* life: in dream interpretation, as we pointed out earlier, the completed fabric, cut off from the loom, signifies death.[8] This representation of the individual, who is born a thread and dies a fabric, is in keeping with the political "weaving" that we studied at some length at the beginning of this book. For it is by the crossing of threads—of opposite directions and sexes—that the fabric of society is created, starting with the elementary interlacing that is the sexual union of two individuals.

Thus this metaphorical weaving is unlike that found in

the verse of the Psalms quoted earlier. It does not fit with the notion of biological fabric: one might even think that it was an *obstacle* to the formation of such a notion, for, according to the weaving of destiny, in Greece and Rome, it is not at the start of his existence but only at the end that the individual becomes a "fabric," even though all the threads are meticulously prepared in advance by the Moirai or the Parcae. Therefore, if we wish to find precedents for what we call "body tissues," we are obliged to seek elsewhere—specifically in the current of thought that subscribes to the theory of metempsychosis or reincarnation.

"The Egyptians are . . . the first to have stated the doctrine that the soul of man is immortal," says Herodotus, "that, when the body perishes, it enters [*esduetai*] another animal that is being born in turn; that, having run through all the beings of the earth, the sea, and the air, it again enters [*esdunein*] the body of a man being born."[9] As for the Greeks who made this doctrine their own, the historian prefers to remain silent, but one name comes easily to mind: that of Pythagoras; for, as we learn in Xenophanes, the philosopher of Samos firmly believed in reincarnation.[10] Later these very Pythagorean theories would be at issue when Aristotle took the notion of metempsychosis to task: "As though it were possible . . . for any soul to find its way [*enduesthai*] into any body."[11]

But the Pythagoreans were not the only ones to believe in reincarnation. A long Greek tradition, which included Pindar[12] as well as Plato, adopted the Egyptian theory. In the eschatological myth of *The Republic* the visitor of the underworld sees, among other things, the soul of Thersites: "Far off, among the last, [he saw] the buffoon Thersites' soul clothing itself in the body of an ape [*pithēkon enduome-nēn*]."[13] Previously, on the subjects of King Endymion and the *Eudumatia*, we focused sufficiently on the verb *enduein* that its vestimentary meaning should not go unnoticed: in Greek, in effect, one can *enduesthai* a garment—for example, a *stolē*[14]—as well as a body. This manner of speaking seems to imply that the soul uses the body as a "garment," donning it upon returning from the underworld. In any case this is what Empedocles—whose soul had gone through several reincarnations[15]—asserts in a fragment in which he speaks of Nature (or a similar subject) "who dresses [*per-istellousa*] (souls) with a new coat of flesh [*sarkōn . . . chitōni*]."[16] The verb used by Empedocles—*peristellein*—is just as garment-related as *enduesthai;* indeed, the noun *stolē*, "dress," is derived from it. But in the fragment cited, souls are dressed in a *chitōn*, a fact that may be significant.[17]

Once developed, the idea of the body-fabric can become autonomous with respect to the theory of reincarnation, to the point that the body will become a fabric even for an anti-Pythagorean such as Heraclitus.[18] In his work the analogy takes a rather specific form; the fabric to which the body is compared is a spider's web:[19] "Just as the spider posted at the center of the web instantly senses that a fly is stuck to one of its threads and hastens to it, as if suffering from the break in the thread, so man's soul, if some part of the body is wounded, hurries to it, as if unable to bear the wound to the body, to which it is firmly joined and in harmony."[20]

Whereas in Heraclitus the soul weaves and reweaves its body like a spider, in Plato's *Phaedo* it becomes a weaver—a human and male weaver. Cebes develops an image by which he wishes to prove that the soul, weaving and reweaving its body in the manner of a *huphantēs*, can no longer survive once it is separated from its final "garment."[21] The soul is thus enveloped by the body as by a garment (which it manufactures itself).

Though used in an entirely different sense, the same image is also found in the *Gorgias*, in which Socrates explains how the dead are judged. In days past, he says, the judges were living men who decided the fate of the dead the very day they died. This was the case until Zeus found himself forced to reform the entire institution: "I shall put an end to this evil," says the god. "If judgments have been poorly made, it is because men are judged while still dressed [*ampekhomenoi*], for they are judged while still alive. Now many men with sickly souls are covered [*emphiesmenoi*] with beautiful bodies . . . The judges also pass judgment while dressed [*amphekhomenoi*], with their soul, eyes, ears, an entire body surrounding them . . . Men must be judged naked, and therefore must be judged after their death. The judge, too, must be naked and dead."[22]

Thus Plato is perfectly familiar with the metaphor of corporeal fabric, prefiguring the more recent notion of histology. Indeed, this notion resurfaces in the *Timaeus*. The first relevant passage we quote from this dialogue adds nothing really new with respect to the examples we have just read: "For the rest," says the Demiurge to the gods, "adding, by weaving [*proshuphainontes*], a mortal part to this immortal part, fabricate Living Beings, give them life, food, make them grow, and, when they perish, welcome them again next to you."[23]

It is in a passage devoted to the spleen that the metaphor

of biological weaving makes its definitive appearance, so to speak: "When impurities are produced in the liver as a result of illnesses of the body, the porosity of the spleen purifies them by taking them in, for it absorbs them because its fabric is hollow and bloodless [*hate koilou kai anaimou huphanthentos*]."[24]

Appendix B

NOTE ON COSMIC "WEAVING"

A CONTEMPORARY of Catullus and of Cicero, Lucretius lived at a time when the metaphor of scriptural *texere*, designating the "weaving" of a written work, had become common in Rome.[1] This concept of written or poetic composition could hardly have been unknown to the author of *De rerum natura*. Although Lucretius nowhere explicitly says that he is "weaving" his poem or that it constitutes a metaphorical "fabric," one of his followers, the author of the *Ciris*, imagines his own poem devoted "to the nature of things" *(naturae rerum)* as a great Panathenaean *peplos*, "woven" to the glory of his patron Messalla.[2] Given that the follower speaks of "weaving" his poem for his patron, there is nothing strange in thinking that the great master—who was in fact very knowledgeable about the techniques of weaving[3]—did the same for the glory of Memmius, even though he doesn't say so explicitly.

The metaphor of weaving comes forcefully into play on several occasions in Lucretius, but in the nominal form rather than in the form of the verb *texere*.[4] In the tradition of Greek materialist philosophy, which since Leucippus and Democritus had considered physical reality a *sumplokē*,[5] the Latin poet-philosopher sees the "atomic structure" as a *textura*, a *textum*, or a *textus*.[6] This metaphor, however, cannot be unrelated to alphabetic writing. For the "elements" that join together as if united into a fabric in the physical world are first and foremost, both in Greek and in Latin, the "elements" of writing.[7] The Greek *stoicheia* are the Latin *elementa:* both words refer to "alphabetic signs" as well as to "atoms," with the first meaning historically preceding the second. Which is to say that the sense of "atom" was derived from that of "letters"; the physical world was interpreted in terms of the alphabetic model (and not vice versa).[8] The *sumplokē* of letters, which we studied in Plato,[9] should thus be considered as the intermediary between weaving properly speaking and the metaphor of weaving *elementa* into a *textus* of atoms. This is all the more significant because, unlike the *grammata*, the *stoicheia* ideally constitute alphabetic signs in that they form an intelligible *sequence*—that is, signs that have undergone *sumplokē* and are joined together.[10]

Once this genealogy of the "elements" is recognized, it becomes easier to accept our hypothesis regarding the "woven" status of Lucretius' poem. Yet the decisive fact here is situated on a level other than that of the relation between metaphors. For should we not assume that the materialist poet considered his own poem as part of "things" *(res)* and, as such, subject to the same laws as the rest of the universe? This, in any case, is our view. For Lucretius, the poem must inevitably be part of the world he describes. Thus it is itself a *textus*, even though it is not so for the same reasons we have already encountered elsewhere. These reasons can be clarified by a rereading of the famous prologue to *De rerum natura*.

Although it is wrong to see Lucretius as an "atheist,"[11] the invocation to Venus, which opens *De rerum natura*, has nevertheless understandably left more than one reader perplexed. How could the materialist poet, an unconditional enemy of traditional religion,[12] address a Venus so un-"philosophical" in appearance but, on the other hand, definitively Latin, since she is characterized from the start as *Aeneadum genetrix*, "mother of the descendants of Aeneas"?[13] How could the Epicurean philosopher, for whom the gods inhabit the *intermundia* far from men,[14] appeal to this Venus without falling into the most flagrant contradiction? What is the purpose of this quasi-lyrical passage, a true little hymn to joy, at the very threshold of his austere poem? Of course, these questions have already elicited a number of explanations: the ascendancy of Memmius, to whom the poem is addressed and who is allegedly descended from the goddess; the influence of poetic or rhetorical conventions, to which on this one occasion the poet yielded in order to furnish a bright pediment to the edifice of his poem, thereby attracting the reader's interest; and, finally, the possibility of an allegorical representation.[15] In short, the preamble has been absolved for not being in conformity with the poem, as if Lucretius had not really been serious in opening his great text with an invocation to the goddess of love.

But such a position is hardly tenable. After proclaiming the omnipresence of Venus—in the sky, in the sea, and on earth[16]—and her absolute power in matters of procreation, Lucretius says: "And since you alone suffice to govern nature and without you nothing may approach the divine banks of light, nothing joyous or pleasant is created, I would like you to join me as my ally when I write these verses [*te sociam studeo scribendis uersibus esse*] . . . In addition, O Divine one, may you give what I say [*dictis*] an eternal beauty."[17] Although Lucretius mentions the Muses later in book 1,[18] he does not do so at the moment when a Homer would have, at the start of his undertaking. It is as if the Muse had been replaced by Venus. For she is the one who will ensure the *sumplokē* of the poem, just as she already ensures that of living beings and physical elements. Venus, whose relationship to speech is not normally very pronounced (as the divinity of weddings, Aphrodite needs Hermes to establish verbal communication between the spouses),[19] becomes in some sense the "Muse of the Written Word": it is thanks to her unifying intervention that Lucretius' poem will hold together durably. If this Venus, by the very place she occupies in the poem, is reminiscent of Sappho's Aphrodite *poikilothronos*—who also is placed ostentatiously at the threshold of the "complete works" and who also qualifies as an "ally"[20]—or of the Aphrodite of the *Homeric Hymn*,[21] the fact remains that we have a theological rupture in Lucretius, a rupture that is the logical consequence of the fact that the Roman's poetics were subject to the laws of his physical science.

In Greece, the power of "interlacing" specific to Aphrodite, that is, the power to knot, to join together, is in a certain manner under the control of Athena: the cr/ of "bonds" in the city cannot be entrusted to Aph. alone. Athena, not Aphrodite, is a weaver. And this is true despite the strongly sexual symbolism of the loom. Now, it is precisely from this type of civic theology, it seems to us, that Lucretius is breaking away when he gives his "creative nature" *(natura creatrix)*, his Venus *Physica*,[22] her full powers—down to the union of letters into syllables and of words into discourse. If in the *Homeric Hymn to Hermes* the passing god is himself present as a rhetorical principle—thanks to which the "passing" is manifested in the very words of the text[23]—Lucretius' Venus is also "present" not only in the prologue but in the entire poem *De rerum natura*. She is the force that holds the poem together. She is everywhere present. The prologue thus turns out to be the enactment of the generating myth of the *sumplokē*, perfectly (and thus philosophically) in place in this *poem* on the *world*. The poetics of the poem on the "nature of things" are but the poetics of the world itself: cosmos and poem obey the same principle, participating in the same logic of "textual" interweaving.

NOTES

Introduction

1. In antique thought, weaving and fabric tend to form a continuum. This is how we envisage them here. In Homer the product is never clearly distinguished from its fabrication: for example, at the very moment when Pandarus draws his arrow, Homer recounts how the weapon was made, with details about the material used and making mention of the artisan (*Iliad* 4.105–111; hereafter cited as *Il.*). Thus the product is not experienced as something that has been definitively separated—by the market—from its process of production. Similarly, the fabric *reminds us* of the weaving (*Il.* 5.338, 734–735; 6.288–292; 14.178–179; 22.510–511).

2. J. Svenbro, *La parole et le marbre. Aux origines de la poétique grecque* (Thesis, Lund, 1976), especially pp. 44–45, 191–192, and 202–204.

3. This was already the case in the document titled "Le tissu du mariage" (1977), cited by N. Loraux, *Les enfants d'Athéna* (Paris: François Maspero, 1981), p. 182 n. 105; translated by C. Levine as *The Children of Athena* (Princeton: Princeton University Press, 1993). Hav-

ing sat for a long time in a drawer, this document served as our point of departure when we began our joint research in 1985. Its perspective owes a great deal to discussions with Britt-Marie Fridh in Rome in 1976–77.

4. J. Scheid and J. Svenbro, "Byrsa. La ruse d'Elissa et la fondation de Carthage," *Annales E.S.C.*, 40 (1985), 328–342.

5. See *Annuaire de L'Ecole Pratique des Hautes Etudes*, 5th Section, 94–96 (1985–86, 1986–87, 1987–88).

6. On this subject, see G. Dumézil, *Mythe et épopée*, vol. 1 (Paris: Gallimard, 1968), pp. 10–11 and passim.

7. At the outset it was our friend Jean-Louis Durand, a Hellenist and Africanist, who suggested this manner of envisioning myth to us. We hope we did not distort his thought in the pursuit of our own work.

8. To take one example: "Moulting is old age." This is the concatenation—liable to bewilder the outsider but familiar to members of the culture in question—sustaining the mythology of the cicada (as well as that of Tithonos) and with a linguistic fact as its point of departure, both in Greek and in Latin. For *geras* and *senectus* signify, in their respective languages, both "moulting" and "old age": to shed one's skin is in some sense to reach an ageless existence (see Callimachus, "Answer to the Telchines," *Aitia* 1, frag. 1.33–35 Pfeiffer). *Bursa*, the "ox-skin" city, is another example of this type of myth. In our article on Byrsa cited in note 4 above, we tried to show how the Greco-Roman imagination, regularly associating the bovine species with the foundation of cities, created the story about the founding of Byrsa by Queen Elissa (Dido): whatever the true name of the city (Bosra? Birtu?), it suggested to the Greek ear that it was called *Bursa*, which, as a result, was attributed a founding story in which an "ox skin" plays the principal role (thanks to a *bursa* cut into strips, Elissa obtains the territory necessary for the foundation of Bursa). *Troia*, as we shall see, is a third example, discreetly combining the notion of the "city" *(Troia)* with that of "weaving" (*troia* meaning "woof").

9. R. Barthes, *Mythologies* (Paris: Seuil, 1957), p. 215; translated by A. Lavers as *Mythologies* (New York, Farrar Straus, 1972).

10. M. Detienne, "L'olivier: Un mythe politico-religieux," in M. I. Finley, ed., *Problèmes de la terre en Grèce ancienne* (Paris and The

Hague: Mouton, 1973), pp. 293–306, reprinted under the title "Un éphèbe, un olivier," in M. Detienne, *L'écriture d'Orphée* (Paris: Gallimard, 1989), pp. 71–84 and 199–204. Detienne's important book *L'invention de la mythologie* (Paris: Gallimard, 1981) deals with quite a different set of problems.

11. It is impossible to imagine that political thought existed, complete and structured, at the dawn of Greek civilization, awaiting the explicator capable of finding the metaphor best adapted to making it intelligible. On the contrary, it structured itself *through* the metaphor, through the "handmade" and its elementary symbolism, well before Plato wrote *The Statesman*.

12. M. Guarducci, "Il conubium nei riti del matrimonio etrusco e di quello romano," *Bullettino della Commissione archeologica communale di Roma*, 55 (1927), 205–224; J.-M. Moret, "Circé tisseuse sur les vases de Cabirion," *Revue archéologique*, 2 (1991), 227–266. Aside from these two bibliographical landmarks, we should mention B.-M. Fridh-Haneson, *Le manteau symbolique. Etude sur les couples votifs en terre cuite assis sous un même manteau* (Stockholm: Paul Åströms Förlag, 1983); G. Arrigoni, "Amore sotto il manto e iniziazione nuziale," *Quaderni Urbinati di cultura classica*, 3 (1983), 7–56; H.-G. Buchholz, "Das Symbol des gemeinsamen Mantels," *Mitteilungen des Deutschen archäologischen Instituts. Römische Abteilung*, 102 (1987), 1–55; G. Koch-Harnack, *Erotische Symbole. Lotosblüte und gemeinsamer Mantel auf antiken Vasen* (Berlin: Gabr. Mann Verlag, 1989), pp. 109–185. E. Gullberg and P. Åström, *The Thread of Ariadne: A Study of Ancient Greek Dress*, Studies in Mediterranean Archaeology, 21 (Göteborg: Paul Åströms Förlag, 1970), fits more into the domain of the *realia*, in the tradition of H. Blümner, "Das Weben," in *Technologie und Terminologie der Gewerbe und Künste bei Griechen und Römern*, vol. 1 (1912; reprint, Hildesheim: Georg Olms Verlagsbuchhandlung, 1969), pp. 135–170. To this short bibliography we should also add I. Papdopoulou-Belmehdi, *L'art de Pandora: La mythologie du tissage en Grèce ancienne* (Thesis under the direction of N. Loraux, Ecole des Hautes Etudes en Sciences Sociales, Paris, 1992), which adopts a perspective fairly close to our own while arriving at very different conclusions (considering weaving, on a symbolic level, as a representation of the "virgin state").

13. Plato, *Statesman* 283b.

14. P. Bourdieu, *Le sens pratique* (Paris: Editions du Minuit, 1980), p. 27.

15. See C. Kluckhohn and D. Leighton, *The Navaho*, ed. L. H. Wales and R. Kluckhohn (Garden City, N.Y.: Natural History Library and Doubleday/Anchor, 1962), p. 306: "Many women will not weave more than about two hours at a stretch; in the old days unmarried girls were not allowed to weave for fear they would overdo, and there is a folk rite for curing the results of excess in this activity. Closely related to this is the fear of completely finishing anything . . . the weaver leaves a small slit between the threads . . . Singers also systematically leave out transitions in relating myths."

1. From the Sixteen Women to the Weaver King

1. For Greek sacrifice, see first of all M. Detienne and J.-P. Vernant, *La cuisine du sacrifice en pays grec* (Paris: Gallimard, 1979), translated by P. Wissing as *The Cuisine of Sacrifice among the Greeks* (Chicago: University of Chicago Press, 1989). For Roman sacrifice, J. Scheid, "La spartizione sacrificale a Roma," in C. Grottanelli and N. Parise, eds., *Sacrificio e società nel mondo antico* (Rome and Bari: Laterza, 1988), pp. 267–292.

2. The metaphor of the ship of state is found in archaic poetry: see Alcaeus, frags. 6 and 326 Lobel-Page, with commentary by D. L. Page, *Sappho and Alcaeus*, 2nd ed. (Oxford: Clarendon Press, 1955), pp. 181–189; Theognis 667–682; also Aeschylus, *Seven against Thebes* 1–3, 62–64, 208–210, and 652 (see Z. Petre, "Thèmes dominants et attitudes politiques dans *Les sept contre Thèbes* d'Eschyle," *Studii clasice*, 13 [1971], 16 and n. 6); Plato, *Republic* 488a–489b, etc.

3. Pausanias, *Description of Greece* 5.16.2–3, trans. W. H. S. Jones (Cambridge, Mass.: Loeb Classical Library, Harvard University Press, 1926; cited hereafter as Pausanias). For the Sixteen Women, see the recent study by C. Calame, "Pausanias le périégète en ethnographe ou comment décrire un culte grec," in J.-M. Adam, M.-J. Borel, C. Calame, and M. Kilani, *Le discours anthropologique* (Paris: Méridiens Klincksieck, 1990), pp. 234–246; also M. Detienne, "Violentes 'eugé-

nies,'" in Detienne and Vernant, *La cuisine*, pp. 188–189. For the Dionysian aspect of the cult of the Sixteen Women, see M. Detienne, *Dionysos à ciel ouvert* (Paris: Hachette, 1986), pp. 84–87; translated by A. Goldhammer as *Dionysos at Large* (Cambridge, Mass.: Harvard University Press, 1989), pp. 55–56.

4. This seems to be the double of another Damophon, who in 588 B.C. initiated a process that would lead to the destruction of Pisa (and to the erection of the temple and of the statue of Zeus at Olympus): Pausanias 6.22.3–4 (and 5.10.2).

5. Pausanias 5.16.5–6.

6. Pausanias 3.16.2. The connection is made by L. Gernet, *Anthropologie de la Grèce antique* (Paris: François Maspero, 1968), p. 202, in a passage that at one time served as our point of departure (pp. 201–204). See also L. Bruit Zaidman, "Pandora's Daughters and Rituals in Grecian Cities," in G. Duby and M. Perrot, eds., *A History of Women in the West*, vol. 1: *From Ancient Goddesses to Christian Saints*, ed. P. Schmitt Pantel, trans. A. Goldhammer (Cambridge, Mass.: The Belknap Press of Harvard University Press, 1992).

7. Pausanias 6.24.10.

8. Pausanias 5.16.7.

9. Artemidorus, *Interpretation of Dreams* 3.36.

10. Diodorus 11.54.1: *mikrai poleis*.

11. Leander, *FGrHist* 492 F 13: *komai* (see Strabo 8.3.2).

12. Document on the synoecism of Elis in M. Moggi, *I sinecismi interstatali greci*, vol. 1 (Pisa: Marlin, 1976), pp. 157–166.

13. Plutarch, *Life of Theseus* 24.1–3; see also Moggi, *I sinecismi*, pp. 1–5 and 44–81. The equivalence between *dēmos* (Attic) and *kōmē* (Dorian) is posited by Aristotle, *Poetics* 1448a37.

14. See, for example, M. Detienne, *Les jardins d'Adonis* (Paris: Gallimard, 1972), p. 171; translated by J. Lloyd as *The Garden of Adonis* (Princeton: Princeton University Press, 1993).

15. Pausanias 5.17.1.

16. Pausanias 5.16.4.

17. For the vocabulary of weaving, see H. Blümner, *Technologie und Terminologie der Gewerbe und Künste bei den Griechen und Römern*, vol. 1 (1912; reprint, Hildesheim: Georg Olms Verlagsbuchhandlung,

1969), pp. 135–170, especially pp. 141–142 (for the terms in question here).

18. Aristotle, *Generation of Animals* 717a34–36, 787b190–26, 788a305. See Blümner, *Technologie und Terminologie*, p. 146 and n. 2.

19. Orpheus, frag. B 22, in H. Diels and W. Kranz, *Fragmente der Vorsokratiker*, vol. 3, 6th ed. (Berlin: Weidmann, 1951; hereafter cited as Diels-Kranz); *Orphicorum Fragmenta*, frag. 33 Kern.

20. Seneca, *Letters* 90.20. See Chapter 4, text at note 21.

21. The word *sumplokē* designates both the union of the warp and the woof in weaving (see Plato, *Statesman* 281a) and the sexual union of the man and woman (see Plato, *Symposium* 191c).

22. For the double meaning of *sunoikismos*, see Plutarch, *Life of Solon* 20.6 (matrimonial cohabitation) and *Life of Romulus* 9.4 (political cohabitation; compare *Life of Theseus* 24.1, in which the verb *sunoikizein* has the same ambiguity).

23. Peter J. Wilson points out that Pelops is an anagram of *peplos*.

24. Pausanias 5.16.6; for the other Dionysian chorus, called Physkoa, see first Calame, "Pausanias le périégète," pp. 237–238 and 242–244, citing, among others, L. Weniger, *Das Kollegium der Sechzehn Frauen und der Dionysosdienst in Elis* (Weimar, 1883).

25. Ibycus, frag. 3 Page; Pausanias 5.8.1.

26. *The Scholia to Apollonius Rhodius, Argonautica* 4.57–58. See *The Scholia to Theocritus, Idylls* 3.49–51b.

27. Pausanias 5.8.1.

28. See the scholia cited in note 26, as well as Apollodorus, *Bibliotheca* 1.7.5. An epigram by Meleager (*Anthologia Palatina* 5.165) seems to play on the vestimentary meaning of the name Endymion: the poet imagines his rival lying *hupo chlainēi*, "under the cloak," of Heliodorus (line 3), "like a second Endymion" (line 6); see Chapter 3, text at note 91.

29. Pausanias 6.19.11.

30. Pausanias 6.20.7 and 9.

31. See first of all N. Loraux, *Les enfants d'Athéna* (Paris: François Maspero, 1981), pp. 188–189; translated by C. Levine as *The Children of Athens* (Princeton: Princeton University Press, 1993). For a recent

commentary on the passage in question (lines 565–588), see also J. Henderson, *Aristophanes' Lysistrata* (Oxford: Clarendon Press, 1987), pp. 141–145, who in connection with the metaphor of weaving cites W. Hugill, *Panhellenism in Aristophanes* (Chicago: Chicago University Press, 1936), and C. Moulton, *Aristophanic Poetry,* Hypomnemata, 68 (Göttingen: Vandenhoeck & Ruprecht, 1981).

32. Aristophanes, *Lysistrata* 565–570.

33. Ibid., 574–576.

34. Ibid., 577–578. For U. von Wilamowitz-Moellendorff (*Aristophanes. Lysistrata* [1927; reprint, Berlin-Zürich, Weidmann, 1964] pp. 157–158), the word *sunhistamenoi* evokes *stasis,* "civil strife"; given the context, it also evokes *histos,* "loom, cloth," derived from the same verb as *stasis.* We will return to this later.

35. Aristophanes, *Lysistrata* 579–581.

36. Ibid., 582–584.

37. Ibid., 584–586. See also 1155.

38. The opposition weaving/war is as old as Homer: see *Il.* 6.490–492. Compare *The Scholia to Nicander, Theriaca* 12a, p. 40 Crugnola, on Arachne and Phalanx, weaver and warrior, respectively, transformed into animals after having committed incest (see Chapter 6, note 1).

39. *Il.* 6.269–303.

40. *Il.* 6.304–311.

41. *Il.* 6.288–295.

42. For information about cranes and the beginning of the season of labor, see Hesiod, *Works and Days* 448–451, *Theogony* 1197–1202; and Aristophanes, *Birds* 710–712, in which the cries of the crane are the signal for the peasants to sow, for the mariner to underhand his rudder, and for the bandit to weave a cloak of wool so as not to be cold in winter (agriculture, navigation, and weaving thus follow the same signal). Hesiod's verses on the crane should be compared to *Works and Days* 383–385, in which the beginning of work is determined by the setting of the Pleiades, theoretically on October 31 (according to M. L. West, *Hesiod: Works and Days* [Oxford: Clarendon Press, 1978], p. 256; see p. 380); in practice the date could fall a full week

later, if one were to follow Hippocrates, *Regimen* 3.68 (who situates their setting with respect to the autumnal equinox and the winter solstice).

43. See L. Deubner, *Attische Feste*, 2nd ed. (Berlin: Akademie-Verlag, 1956), pp. 11–12, 23, 31 and 36. Whereas the period of nine months evokes the period of *gestation*, the completion of the work coincides with the day celebrating the *birth* of the goddess.

44. Ibid., pp. 31 and 35–36.

45. *Corpus Paroemiographorum Graecorum*, I.22.13–16 (Zenobius 1.56) Leutsch-Schneidewin: "'An Akeseus and Helikon job!' This proverb applies to marvelous works. For these two men were the first to fabricate *(dēmiourgein)* the peplos of Athena Polias, Akeseus being a native of Patara, Helikon of Karystos." As Pierre Vidal-Naquet points out, Akeseus and Helikon are not Athenian citizens, a fact that heightens the almost shocking nature of this male weaving. For a comical inversion of the norm see *Ulysses the Weaver* by Alexis of Thurii (372–270 B.C.), a play cited by Athenaeus 6.240c, etc. (= frags. 155–157 in *Comicorum Atticorum Fragmenta*, II, pp. 354–355 Kock). See note 75 below.

46. Aristophanes, *Birds* 826–828, with the scholium to line 827; Pausanias 1.26.6. See Deubner, *Attische Feste*, pp. 29–30 (and also pp. 17–18 for the ritual washing of the statue and of its garment on the occasion of the Plynteria).

47. See Plato, *Euthyphro* 6b–c and *Republic* 378b–c; [Virgil], *Ciris* 21–34. See also Aristotle, *Constitution of Athens* 49.3.

48. *The Scholia to Aristides*, p. 323 Dindorf: the Small Panathenaeas were reputedly celebrated "to commemorate the elimination of the giant Asterius by Athena," *epi Asteri toi giganti hupo Athēnaias anairethenti;* scholium cited by R. Eisler, *Weltmantel und Himmelszelt*, vol. 1 (Munich: C. H. Beck, 1910), p. 178, which, however, questions the existence of a giant by this name. In the gigantomachy recounted by Apollodorus, it is the giants Enkelados and Pallas who are killed by the goddess (*Bibliotheca* 1.6.2). In Troy, Athena received a peplos that "shone like a star [*aster*]" (*Il.* 6.295); could such a comparison have "given birth" to Asterius?

49. As observed by Deubner, *Attische Feste*, pp. 22–23, citing Pausanias 8.2.1.

50. See Plutarch, *Life of Theseus* 24.1–3, etc.; see Moggi, *I sinecismi*, pp. 44–81.

51. See Deubner, *Attische Feste*, p. 30 and n. 9 (quoting J. N. Svoronos).

52. The Greek terms are taken from a severely damaged inscription from the Acropolis in Athens dating from the mid-fifth century B.C.: *Supplementum Epigraphicum Graecum*, XIV.3.11 (see J. G. Frazer, *Pausanias's Description of Greece*, vol. 2 [1898; reprint, New York: Biblio and Tannen, 1965], p. 574, n. 7); in reality, we do not have precise documents regarding the investiture of the statue of Athena. See M. Bieber, "Two Attic Black-Figured *Lekythoi* in Buffalo," *American Journal of Archaeology*, 48 (1944), 121–129.

53. Deubner, *Attische Feste*, p. 34.

54. Ibid., pp. 24–28.

55. See note 2 above.

56. See J. Svenbro, "A Mégara Hyblaea: Le corps géomètre," *Annales E.S.C.*, 37 (1982), 958 and n. 70.

57. Plutarch, *Life of Themistocles* 4.4.

58. On Athena, patroness of weaving: Hesiod, *Works and Days* 64 (see F. Frontisi-Ducroux, *Dédale: Mythologie et l'artisan en Grèce ancienne* [Paris: François Maspero, 1975], p. 62); on the plow: *Works and Days* 429–431 (see M. Detienne and J.-P. Vernant, *Les ruses de l'intelligence: La mètis des Grecs* [Paris: Flammarion, 1972], pp. 168–169).

59. See Detienne and Vernant, *Les ruses*, pp. 201–241.

60. Document in Deubner, *Attische Feste*, pp. 32–34 (see in particular p. 32 and n. 4).

61. We are thinking in particular of the votive reliefs of Locri Epizephyrii that depict *peplophoria:* see H. Prückner, "Peplophorie und Gewandprozession," in *Die lokrischen Tonreliefs. Bietrag zue Kultgeschichte von Lokroi Epizephyrioi* (Mainz am Rhein: Ph. von Zabern, 1968), pp. 42–45.

62. See C. Calame, *Les choeurs de jeunes filles en grèce archaïque*, vol. 2 (Rome: Edizioni dell'Ateneo & Bizzarri, 1977), pp. 128–130.

63. See C. Segal, "Sirius and the Pleiades in Alcman's Louvre Partheneion," *Mnemosyne*, 36 (1983), 260–275; also C. Calame, *Alcman: Introduction, texte critique, témoignages, traduction et commentaire* (Rome: Edizioni dell'Ateneo, 1983), pp. 331–334.

64. Or perhaps "like the Sun"; see Hesychius, s.v. *Seirios:* "Archilochus thus designates the sun" (Archilochus, frag. 85 Bonnard-Lasserre).

65. Alcman, frag. 1.60–63 Page.

66. Aside from *Il.* 6.289, we should mention *Odyssey* 15.108 (cited hereafter as *Od.*); see also Apollonius Rhodius, *Argonautica* 1.725–726. In our opinion, one must avoid the interpretation that takes *Peléades* with *hate Sērion*—as if a constellation, even figuratively, needed to be compared to a star (see Segal, who is of another opinion, in "Sirius and the Pleiades," p. 270 n. 30).

67. Bacchylides, *Victory Odes* 5.9–10.

68. See Deubner, *Attische Feste*, p. 34. For the "myth of the olive tree," see the remarkable article by M. Detienne, "L'olivier: Un mythe politico-religieux," in M. I. Finley, ed., *Problèmes de la terre en Grèce ancienne* (Paris and The Hague: Mouton, 1973), pp. 293–306; reprinted as "Un éphèbe, un olivier," in M. Detienne, *L'écriture d'Orphée* (Paris: Gallimard, 1989), pp. 71–84 and 199–204. Planted at designated distances (Plutarch, *Life of Solon* 23.7), olive trees incarnate citizen-warriors in the order of battle and thus lend themselves to a symbolism that is both social and spatial. If the metaphor of fabric does not seem to possess this two-pronged orientation, we should recall that the surveyor's cords, used to trace the reticular plan of an archaic city upon its foundation (see Callimachus, "The Foundation of Zancle," *Aetia* 2, frag. 43.63–65 Pfeiffer), may evoke the texture of a fabric, in which the threads of the warp and the woof cross at right angles. Later on, the plan of Alexandria took the shape of a garment, namely that of a chlamys (Plutarch, *Life of Alexander* 26.5).

69. Plato, *Statesman* 287c (*temnein*, "to cut," and *diairein*, "to divide," are terms that occur fairly frequently in this dialogue), 296e–297a.

70. See Henderson, who, in his edition of *Lysistrata* (p. 142: "Lysistrata's metaphor may well have inspired those of Plato in *Pol.*

308C–D, 310E, 311B–E"), refers to P. Louis, *Les métaphores de Platon* (Paris: Les Belles Lettres, 1945), p. 165. See also Plato, *Republic* 557c, in which the democratic constitution is compared to a *himation poikilon pasin anthesi pepoikilmenon*, "a cloak that is adorned, decorated (literally: woven) with every flower."

71. Alcaeus, frags. 6 and 326 Lobel-Page; Hesiod, *Theogony* 667–682.

72. Plato, *Republic* 488a–489b. See also the passages from Aeschylus cited in note 2 above.

73. Note the swearword and its context: Zas (= Zeus) is a weaver for the pre-Socratic Pherekydes (frag. B 2 Diels-Kranz), as we shall see later (Chapter 3, text at note 56).

74. Plato, *Statesman* 279b, translated by J. B. Skemp in *The Collected Dialogues of Plato*, ed. Edith Hamilton and Huntington Cairns, Bollingen Series 71 (New York: Pantheon Books, 1961).

75. See P. Vidal-Naquet, *Le chasseur noir* (Paris: François Maspero, 1981), p. 294; translated by Andrew Szegedy-Maszak as *The Black Hunter* (Baltimore: Johns Hopkins University Press, 1986). For Arkas (who taught men to "weave a garment," *estheta huphainesthai*) see Pausanias 8.4.1; see *The Scholia to the Iliad*, 23.762a (Pan "the inventor of fabrics," *heuretēs huphasmatōn*); Lucretius, *De rerum natura* 5.1350–60 (men weaving before women). The existence of male Greek weavers seems to be attested by Plato, *Hippias Minor* 368c4 (Hippias of Elis weaving his own clothing), *Phaedo* 87b, and *Republic* 369d *(huphantēs)*, as well as by Aristotle, *Politics* 1291a13 (the same word; see Aeschines 1.97: *poikiltēs anēr*, "weaver of designs"). Conversely, Herodotus emphasizes that unlike in Greece, in Egypt the men weave at home (2.35; see Sophocles, *Oedipus at Colonus* 337–341). The last three references are taken from Eisler, *Weltmantel und Himmelszelt*, p. 199. See also A. Ballabriga, "L'équinoxe de l'hiver," *Annali della Scuola normale superiore di Pisa. Classe di lettere e di filosofia*, 11 (1981), 491, on Hesiod, *Works and Days* 536–538 (weaving as a masculine activity; compare Aristophanes, *Birds* 712); finally W. Thompson, "Weaving: A Man's Work," *Classical World*, 75 (1982), 217–222.

76. Plato, *Statesman* 285d–e.

77. See Vidal-Naquet, *Le chasseur noir*, p. 308.

78. See J. Svenbro, *Phrasikleia: An Anthropology of Reading in Ancient Greece*, trans. J. Lloyd (Ithaca: Cornell University Press, 1993), p. 180 with nn. 74–75.

79. Plato, *Statesman* 278b: the term already prefigures the theme of weaving. See Chapter 5, text at note 41.

80. Ibid., 277d: *paradeigmatos . . . to paradeigma auto dedeeken*, "my example itself needs an example."

81. Ibid., 277e–278d.

82. Ibid., 279b.

83. Ibid., 285d.

84. Ibid., 279d: "Protections are either roofs [*stegasmata*] or blankets [*skepasmata*]."

85. Ibid., 279c–e.

86. Ibid., 280b.

87. Aristophanes, *Birds* 827: "For whom are we going to card [*xainein*] the peplos?"

88. Plato, *Statesman* 281a.

89. Ibid., 281b.

90. Ibid., 282b–c: "half of the operation of the shuttle [*to tēs kekristikēs hēmisu*]" belongs to "[the art] of separating [*tēs . . . diakritikēs*]."

91. Ibid., 283b: *plektikēn einai krokēs kai stēmonos huphantikēn*.

92. Ibid., 287b.

93. Ibid., 287d.

94. Ibid., 289c. See 281a–b.

95. Ibid., 289e.

96. Ibid., 289e–290a.

97. Ibid., 290b.

98. See above at note 51. The mention of the King-Archon may indeed target this priest's "investiture" of the statue, for although he is responsible for a "political *fabric*," this "king" has nothing to do with the "*weaver* king," the true statesman, who will be discussed toward the end of the dialogue. Hence the importance of the distinction.

99. Plato, *Statesman* 290c–d.

100. Ibid., 291c.

101. Ibid., 300e–303b.

102. Ibid., 303b. For the expression, see Hesiod, *Theogony* 91; see also Aristotle, *Politics* 1284a11.

103. Plato, *Statesman* 303b–c.

104. Ibid., 304c–305e.

105. Ibid., 305e: *panta sunhuphainousan orthotata . . . politikēn.*

106. Ibid., 305e.

107. Ibid., 306a–c.

108. Ibid., 306b, 307c, 308b.

109. Ibid., 306c–307d.

110. Ibid., 307d.

111. Ibid., 308a.

112. Ibid., 308d.

113. Ibid., 308e–309a. See *Laws* 5.734e–735a.

114. *Statesman* 309b.

115. Ibid., 309c–310a.

116. Ibid., 309d–e.

117. Ibid., 310a.

118. Ibid., 310c.

119. Ibid., 310b–e.

120. Ibid., 310e; see 310a.

121. Ibid., 310e–311a. This conception of political weaving suits the Greek imagination, which, while considering the interlacing of threads to be a sexual union, does not consider Aphrodite to be a weaver (as pointed out by I. Papdoupulou-Belmehdi, *L'art de Pandora: La mythologie du tissage en Grèce ancienne* [Thesis, Paris, 1992], pp. 270–272, commenting on Nonnus, *Dionysiaca* 24.239–329); political thought would not accept that Aphrodite alone be entrusted with the creation of bonds in the city. Rather Athena is the patroness of weaving, as if it were important to subordinate the sexual symbolism of the *sumplokē* to her, thus avoiding the transformation of the work of weavers into erotic daydreams: see Sappho, frag. 102 Lobel-Page.

122. Plato, *Statesman* 311c.

123. Plutarch, *On Music* 1134c. For Hera's garment, see Hesychius, s.v. *patos*, a word that "also designates Hera's garment [*kai enduma tēs*

Hēras]"; compare Callimachus, *Aetia* 3, frag. 66.2–3 Pfeiffer, who alludes to the weaving of this *patos* devoted to Hera. We will return to this.

124. *Od.* 24.534–535. See J. Svenbro, "Vengeance et société en Grèce archaïque," in R. Verdier and J.-P. Poly, eds., *La vengeance*, vol. 3 (Paris: Editions Cujas, 1984), pp. 47–63.

125. Plato, *Statesman* 309c–310a.

126. Ibid., 306b, 307d, 308b.

127. Ibid., 310b.

128. Pausanias 8.4.1.

129. See Chapter 1, text at note 25.

130. See, for example, Deubner, *Attische Feste*, p. 30.

131. See Calame, "Pausanias le périégète," p. 238, who, on the subject of the Sixteen Women, speaks pertinently of "the cultural and political integration of Elis and Pisa." If the Sixteen Women express this integration by their two-pronged cultural orientation—Heraean and Dionysian—it should be noted that the figure of "the one of the garment," Endymion, is balanced by that of "the one of wine," Oinomaos (for the -*maos* element of this proper name, see P. Chantraine, *Dictionnaire étymologique de la langue grecque* [Paris: Klincksieck, 1968–1980], s.v. *maiomai*, p. 659). Of the former capital of Pisatis, Pisa, where Oinomaos reigned, nothing was left in his day, says Pausanias, who adds that vines had been planted there (6.22.1–2).

2. "Investiture," Peplophoria, Lusus Troiae

1. See H. Diels, *Sibyllinische Blätter* (Berlin: Georg Reimer, 1890), pp. 17–19, quoting, notably, Livy (in Julius Obsequens, 27 and 30 [86 and 90], pp. 159–162 Rossbach).

2. Phlegon of Tralles, *FGrHist*, 257 F 36.10 (for *exhēgeisthai*, "perform the exegesis of," see J. Svenbro, *Phrasikleia: An Anthropology of Reading in Ancient Greece*, trans. J. Lloyd [Ithaca: Cornell University Press, 1993], pp. 117–122). Cf. L. Brisson, "Aspect politique de la bisexualité: L'histoire de Polycrite (Phlégon, *De mirab.*, ch. 2; Proclus, *In Remp.*, II.7–15 Kroll)," in *Hommages à M. J. Vermaseren*, ed. M. B. de Boer and T. A. Edridge (Leiden: Brill, 1978), pp. 80–122.

3. Phlegon, (A) la–29. See Diels, *Sibyllinische Blätter,* pp. 38–39.

4. Phlegon, (B) 30–70. See Diels, *Sibyllinische Blätter,* p. 49. For the relationship of Apollo and Hera to the Cumaean Sibyl, see N. Valenza Mele, "Hera ed Apollo a Cuma e la mantica sibillina," *Rivista dell'Istituto nazionale d'archeologia e storia dell'arte,* 14–15 (1991–92), 5–71.

5. Phlegon, (B) 30–31.

6. Diels, *Sibyllinische Blätter,* p. 19, thinks that the Senate's exceptional publication of the oracle aimed to reassure "good citizens" and to forewarn the "bad."

7. Ibid., pp. 17–18, quoting Appian, *Roman History* 1.34; Valerius Maximus 4.5.1; Plutarch, *Life of Caius Gracchus* 3; Livy in Julius Obsequens, 27 (86), p. 159 Rossbach.

8. Phlegon, (A) 16. See Diels, *Sibyllinische Blätter,* p. 55. The Greek adverb translates the Latin formula *Graeco ritu,* "according to the Greek ritual."

9. See Y. Thomas, "The Division of the Sexes in Roman Law," in G. Duby and M. Perrot, eds., *A History of Women in the West,* vol. 1: *From Ancient Goddesses to Christian Saints,* ed. P. Schmitt-Pantel, trans. A. Goldhammer (Cambridge, Mass.: The Belknap Press of Harvard University Press, 1992), pp. 84–85, which describes how, in Roman law, the hermaphrodite had to be classified as either a male or a female, a third genre being legally inadmissible.

10. While the first oracle says (line 27) that women "must implore" *Ploutōnis* to "stay in the country," *en patrai eukhesthon mimnein,* such a prayer emphasizes the linkage between the goddess and Roman soil. See also Diels, *Sibyllinische Blätter,* p. 77, for whom this expression suggests the possibility of an exile *(Auswanderung)* of the goddess.

11. Silius Italicus, *Punica* 7.77.

12. Ibid., 75–77.

13. *Il.* 6.286–311.

14. Silius Italicus, *Punica* 7.79–83.

15. Ibid., 83–85.

16. See *Il.* 6.303: *epi gounasin.*

17. Diels, *Sibyllinische Blätter,* p. 50: "Das Darbringen von Gewändern ist etwas so gewöhnliches, dass es [in der annalistischen Ueber-

lieferung] keine Erwähnung gefunden hat, sondern wohl miteinbegriffen ist . . . in den Geschenken für Ceres und Proserpina."

18. For the sources, see K. Schneider, "Lusus Troiae," in *Paulys Realencyclopädie der classischen Alktertumswissenschaft*, XIII.2 (Stuttgart, 1927), cols. 2059–67; and, for the bibliography, E. Mehl, "Troiaspiel," ibid., *Supplementband* VIII (Munich, 1956), cols. 888–905; K. W. Weeber, "Troiae Lusus: Alter und Entstehung eines Reiterspiels," *Ancient Society*, 5 (1974), 171–196. One should not forget, in particular because of its diagrams, the old article by F. Rasch, "De ludo Troiae: Commentatio philologica," *Jahresbericht über das Gymnasium Carolo-Alexandrinum*, no. 600 (1882), 1–20.

19. Plutarch, *Life of Cato* 3.1. Weeber, "Troiae Lusus," pp. 190–194, thinks that the game was introduced in Rome by Sulla. We will not enter here into the debate regarding the age of the institution.

20. Dionysius of Halicarnassus, *Roman Antiquities* 2.72.

21. Suetonius, *Life of Divine Augustus* 43.5–7.

22. See Schneider, "Lusus Troiae."

23. H. Kern, *Labyrinthe* (Munich: Prestel Verlag, 1982), pp. 182–183.

24. Ibid.

25. Virgil, *Aeneid* 5.545–602, trans. W. F. Jackson Knight (Harmondsworth: Penguin Books, 1956; cited hereafter as *Aeneid*). Compare Claudian, *Panegyric on the Sixth Consulship of Honorius* 621–639.

26. *Aeneid* 5.583–587. Surprisingly, Weeber, "Troiae Lusus," p. 181, considers that Virgil is not describing a real exercise. See Claudian, *Panegyric* 628–630, 632–633, 636–639 (simulation of combat, battle, and separation).

27. *Aeneid* 5.589–593. In Claudian, the *textae fugae* ("woven flights," *Panegyric* 623) of the *lusus* (621) is also associated with the "Gortynian home of the half-human bull" (634).

28. Servius, *Commentary to the Aeneid* ad loc.

29. Whereas the historian Pherekydes uses *mitos* to designate Ariadne's thread (*The Scholia to the Odyssey* 11.320 = *FGrHist* 3 F 148), Propertius uses the Latin synonym *stamen* (4.4.42; compare 2.14.8: *linum*). See also Catullus 64.113; Ovid, *Heroides* 10.72; *Aeneid* 6.30; Servius, *Commentary to the Aeneid* 6.114.

30. *Aeneid* 5.594–595. See G. Capdeville, "Virgile, le Labyrinthe et les dauphins," in *Res sacrae: Hommages à H. Le Bonnier*, ed. D. Porte and J.-P. Néraudeau (Brussels: Latomus, 1988), pp. 65–82. A recent article on the figure of the labyrinth is G. Dareggi, "I mosaici con raffigurazioni del labirinto: Una variazione sul tema del 'centro,'" *Mélanges de l'École française de Rome, Antiquités*, 104 (1992), 281–292.

31. Euripides, *Helen* 1451–58; see Capdeville, "Virgile, le Labyrinthe et les dauphins," pp. 699 ff. This aspect of the dolphins is all the more significant because dance, as we shall see later, has an analogous relationship to weaving.

32. Aelian, *Nature of Animals* 10.8, 1.18.

33. Ovid, *Metamorphoses* 3.684.

34. *Aeneid* 5.596–601.

35. *Aeneid* 5.602.

36. See Schneider, "Lusus Troiae," col. 2059. Aside from the very recent article by M. Menichetti, "L'*oinochoe* di Tragliatella: Mito e rito tra Grecia ed Etruria," *Ostraka*, 1 (1992), 7–30, we should mention G. Q. Giglioli, "L'oinochoe di Tragliatella," *Studi etruschi*, 3 (1929), 111–159; C. Gallini, "Potinija Daparitoyo," *Acme*, 12 (1959), 156–176; J. Kraft, "The Cretan Labyrinth and the Walls of Troy: An Analysis of the Labyrinth Designs," *Opuscula Romana*, 15 (1985), 79–86; Weeber, "Troiae Lusus," p. 175, with a critical bibliography. Weeber (pp. 179–180) does not accept the hypothesis that the *lusus* is represented on the vase: according to him, the seven circles represent not the labyrinth but the ramparts of a city (p. 185). We should recall, nonetheless, that later on, ramparts surrounding a labyrinth on mosaics represent Rome.

37. Paul the Deacon, p. 9 Lindsay. Weeber, "Troiae Lusus," p. 173, notes that the movement in question is circular.

38. Servius, *Commentary to the Aeneid* 5.603: "As Suetonius Tranquillus [our Suetonius] affirms, the game itself, to which the name Pyrrhic is often given [*quem uulgo pyrrhicam appellant*], is called *Troia*, the origins of which he traces in his book on boys' games." Compare Euripides, *Andromache* 1135–40: "You would have seen the child's terrible war dances [i.e., with reference to Neoptolemus] [*deinas d'an*

eides purrikhas . . . paidos] . . . Leaping with that leap that the Trojans knew [*to Troikon pedema pedesas*], he dashed upon them." Neither the Pyrrhic dance nor the "Trojan leap" relates to an equestrian figure. For the Pyrrhic dance, see P. Dinzelbacher, "Uber Troiaritt und Pyrriche," *Eranos*, 80 (1982), 151–161; P. Vidal-Naquet, "Retour au chasseur noir," in J.-P. Vernant and P. Vidal-Naquet, *La Grèce ancienne*, vol. 3: *Rites de passage et transgression* (Paris: Seuil, 1992), p. 246.

39. *Contra* Weeber, "Troiae Lusus," pp. 174–175.

40. *Glossaria Latina*, II.460.1. See H. G. Liddell, R. Scott, and H. S. Jones, *A Greek-English Lexicon*, 9th ed. (Oxford: Clarendon Press, 1961; cited hereafter as Liddell-Scott-Jones), s.v. *troia*.

41. Hesychius, s.v. *troa*.

42. Weeber, "Troiae Lusus," pp. 172–173.

43. *Aeneid* 5.550, 557, 582, 585–586.

44. *Aeneid* 5.577–587.

45. See the oppositions between the *lusus* and the *proelia* or the *bellum, Aeneid* 5.593 and 674.

46. For example, during the funeral of Drusilla, sister of Caligula, in July 38 (Dio Cassius 59.11.2) or of Septimius Severus in 211 (ibid., 76.5.3, and no doubt Herodian 4.2.9, mentioned by Schneider, "Lusus Troiae," col. 2061).

47. For this ritual, see Ovid, *Fasti* 6.206; Servius, *Commentary to the Aeneid* 9.53; Dio Cassius 71.33.3.

48. See Chapter 1, text accompanying note 108 and the final paragraphs of that chapter.

49. *Aeneid* 5.587. Weeber, "Troiae Lusus," p. 179, has not understood the description in its entirety. Nonetheless he is right to consider that it was not simply a matter of an exercise of skill.

50. *Aeneid* 5.596–597.

51. As noted earlier, we know, for example, that the game was performed during the secular games of 204 and during the funeral of Septimius Severus in 211.

52. Suetonius, *Life of Divine Augustus* 43.7. Unlike Weeber, "Troiae Lusus," p. 194, we believe that the *lusus* had a highly political meaning at this time.

3. *Aphrodite* Poikilothronos

1. Sappho, frag. 1.1 Lobel-Page.

2. Liddell-Scott-Jones, s.v.

3. D. A. Campbell, *Greek Lyric*, vol. 1 (Cambridge, Mass.: Loeb Classical Library, Harvard University Press, 1982), p. 53: "Ornate-throned."

4. See chiefly D. L. Page, *Sappho and Alcaeus: An Introduction to the Study of Ancient Lesbian Poetry*, 2nd ed. (Oxford: Clarendon Press, 1959), p. 5.

5. Ibid.: "The word . . . is not found elsewhere, and the idea expressed in it is not at all common in literature." While M. Treu, writing at the same time as Page, also favors an Aphrodite "auf buntem Throne," he alerts his readers to the alternative interpretation (*Sappho,* 2nd ed. [Munich: Ernst Heimeran Verlag, 1958], p. 176).

6. H. Frisk, *Griechisches etymologisches Wörterbuch*, vol. 1 (Heidelberg, 1960), p. 686; P. Chantraine, *Dictionnaire étymologique de la langue grecque* (Paris: Klincksieck, 1968–1980), p. 442.

7. *Il.* 22.441.

8. L. B. Lawler, "On Certain Homeric Epithets," *Philological Quarterly,* 27 (1948), 80–84.

9. See Aeschylus, *Seven against Thebes* 96 and 319.

10. *The Scholia to Theocritus* 2.59.

11. Hesychius, s.v. *throna.*

12. Ibid., s.v. *trona;* see also s.v. *tronoi:* "[weaving] threads, warp, woof, spindle."

13. U. Von Wilamowitz-Moellendorff, *Sappho und Simonides* (Berlin: Weidmann, 1913), p. 44: "Hier darf wahrlich niemand an *throna poikila* denken: wo wären sie denn?" See G. A. Privitera, "La rete di Afrodite: Ricerche sulla prima ode di Saffo," *Quaderni urbinati di cultura classica,* 4 (1967), 12.

14. Lawler, "On Certain Homeric Epithets," p. 84.

15. See J. Svenbro, "La stratégie de l'amour. Modèle de la guerre et théorie de l'amour dans la poésie de Sappho," *Quaderni di storia,* 19 (1984), 57–79 (and "Sappho and Diomedes," *Museum Philologum Lon-*

diniense, I [1975], 37–49). Also L. Rissmann, *Love as War: Homeric Allusion in the Poetry of Sappho*, Beiträge zur klassischen Philologie, 157 (Königstein: Hein, 1983).

16. Lawler, "On Certain Homeric Epithets," p. 84: *chrusēnios*, "with golden reins," an epithet that, as Privitera ("La rete di Afrodite," p. 12) points out, is perfectly appropriate for a goddess holding reins in her hands.

17. Aristophanes, *Lysistrata* 344.

18. Let us not forget the pioneer in this domain, G. Wustmann, "Die Überlieferung des Plinius über die Anfänge der griechischen Malerei," *Rheinisches Museum*, 23 (1868), 238, n. 50, cited by M. C. J. Putnam, "Throna and Sappho I.1," *Classical Journal*, 56 (1960), 82, n. 3. See also, more recently, F. Lasserre, *Sappho: Une autre lecture* (Padua: Antenore, 1898), p. 240.

19. Privitera, "La rete di Afrodite," p. 12.

20. Diodorus Siculus 16.92.

21. Aristophanes, *Birds* 904–905.

22. Ibid., 936–937.

23. Ibid., 950–951.

24. *Il.* 5.338. For the weaving/fabric relationship, see Introduction, note 1.

25. Athenaeus 15.682e–f, trans. C. Burton Gulick (Cambridge, Mass.: Loeb Classical Library, Harvard University Press, 1941) (= [Homer], *Cypria* 4, p. 119 Allen = frag. 4 Bernabé [whose concordance cites numerous parallels]). For the *Charites*, see *Od.* 8.364–366; for the *Horai* see *Homeric Hymn to Aphrodite* 6.5–6.

26. For *mētis*, see the seminal book by M. Detienne and J.-P. Vernant, *Les ruses de l'intelligence: La mètis des Grecs* (Paris: Flammarion, 1974).

27. *Homeric Hymn to Aphrodite* 5.84–90 (here we are following the text of H. G. Evelyn-White in the Loeb edition, 1914, which, for good reasons, reads *péplon . . . pampoikilon* instead of *hormoi . . . pampoikiloi*).

28. The rich designs of their garments can be studied, for example, on the black-figure kylix Berlin F 3993: see G. Koch-Harnack, *Erotische*

Symbole: Lotosblüte und geinsamer Mantel auf antiken Vasen (Berlin: Gebr. Mann Verlag, 1989), p. 111.

29. *Od.* 14.486–502.

30. *Od.* 14.500.

31. *Od.* 14.501–502.

32. C. H. Whitman, *Homer and the Heroic Tradition* (Cambridge, Mass.: Harvard University Press, 1958), p. 277.

33. See L. Robert, "Recherches épigraphiques," *Revue des études anciennes,* 62 (1960), 334, n. 3 (= *Opera Minora Selecta,* II [Amsterdam: Adolf M. Hakkert, 1969] p. 850, n. 3), which tells us that saffron from Cilicia was used for the goldleafing of marble inscriptions.

34. Ovid, *Metamorphoses* 10.1.

35. *Homeric Hymn to Aphrodite* 5.218–238. The goddess is *chrusothronos* (226) as long as she sleeps with her young husband; when this husband grows old, she leaves the conjugal bed and becomes a simple "goddess," *potnia* (230; see 223).

36. *Il.* 1.609–611, trans. Richmond Lattimore.

37. *Il.* 5.769, 6.108, 8.46, 15.371.

38. E. H. Gombrich, *Art and Illusion* (London and New York: Pantheon, 1960), p. 199.

39. See M. Parry, "Studies in the Epic Technique of Oral Verse-Making, I: Homer and Homeric Style," *Harvard Studies in Classical Philology,* 41 (1930), 84–88 (= *The Making of Homeric Verse: The Collected Papers of Milman Parry,* ed. A. Parry [Oxford: Clarendon Press, 1971], pp. 274–279). See G. Nagy, *The Best of the Achaeans* (Baltimore: Johns Hopkins University Press, 1979), p. 1, for a succinct analysis.

40. See Chapter 1, text at note 3 and the final paragraph.

41. See Chapter 2, text at note 11. We are even justified in thinking that in *Punica* 7.77 Silius Italicus transcribes the Homeric epithet *chrusothronos.*

42. *Il.* 1.517–601.

43. *Od.* 4.304–305.

44. Theocritus, *Idylls* 18.16–19.

45. See Liddell-Scott-Jones, s.v. *chlaina.*

46. *Il.* 3.125–128.

47. *Od.* 15.104–110, 123–129.

48. Theocritus, *Idylls* 18.12–34.

49. Even though, in our opinion, the article *tan* has a weakly possessive sense here: "your blanket" = "the blanket beneath which you are lying"; see also M. Guarducci, "Il conubium," *Bollettino della commissione archeologica comunale di Roma*, 55 (1927), 223, who takes *tan* as equivalent to the Latin *illam*, which would give the translation "beneath the *traditional* nuptial blanket."

50. See, for example, J.-P. Vernant, *Mythe et pensée chez les Grecs*, 4th ed. (Paris: La Découverte, 1985), pp. 173–174.

51. Euripides, frag. 603.4 Nauck².

52. *Od.* 15.126–128.

53. Apollodorus, *Bibliotheca* 3.4.2. For the wedding of Kadmos and Harmonia, see M. Rocchi, *Kadmos e Harmonia: Un matrimonio problematico* (Rome: L'Herma di Bretschneider, 1989).

54. Or "It is said that this was the first wedding gift." For this translation, see Pollux 3.36: "The gifts [*dora*] offered by the husband are called . . . *anakaluptēria;* for this is not only the name of the day when he unveils the bride, but also that of the gifts offered on this day; the *anakaluptēria* are also called *prosphthengteria*, gifts of 'salutation.'" See J. Toutain, "Le rite nuptial de l'anakalupterion," *Revue des études anciennes*, 42 (Mélanges G. Radet) (1940), 345–353. See also Pherekydes, frag. B 1 Diels-Kranz: *geras*, "gift of honor."

55. Frag. B 2 Diels-Kranz; translation by G. S. Kirk and J. E. Raven. See M. L. West, "Three Presocratic Cosmologies," *Classical Quarterly*, 13 (1963), 158–169; idem, *Early Greek Philosophy and the Orient* (Oxford: Clarendon Press, 1971); and, more recently, H. S. Schibli, *Pherekydes of Syros* (Oxford: Clarendon Press, 1990), pp. 50–77.

56. Porphyrius, *Life of Pythagoras* 1.17.14–15 Nauck. See M. Detienne, *Homère, Hésiode et Pythagore*, Collection Latomus, 57 (Brussels and Berchem: Latomus, 1962), p. 18.

57. Pherekydes, frag. A 11 Diels-Kranz.

58. Pherekydes, frag. B 2 (from Clement of Alexandria): "the

winged Oak and the richly woven cloak on it," *hē hupopteros drus kai to ep' autēi pepoikilmenon pharos.*

59. Hesiod, *Works and Days* 628 (see the note by M. L. West, *Hesiod: Works and Days* [Oxford: Clarendon Press, 1978], p. 315); Pindar, *Olympian Odes* 9.24.

60. See the critical apparatus of frag. B 2 (H. Diels, cited by W. Kranz).

61. The expression is from Pindar, *Olympian Odes* 7.4.

62. For nuptial ceremonies see, for example, C. M. Bowra, *Greek Lyric Poetry*, 2nd ed. (Oxford: Clarendon Press, 1961), pp. 214–217.

63. Pherekydes, frag. B 3 Diels-Kranz. For cosmic "weaving," see Appendix B.

64. See Chapter 1, note 73.

65. *Statesman* 279d. See Chapter 1, text at note 84.

66. This was a hypothesis formulated by one of us in the document cited by N. Loraux, *Les enfants d'Athéna* (Paris: François Maspero, 1981), p. 182, n. 105; translated by C. Levine as *The Children of Athena* (Princeton: Princeton University Press, 1993). *Contra* G. Arrigioni, "Amore sotto il manto e iniziazione nuziale," *Quaderni urbinati di cultura classica*, 15 (1983), 13.

67. Artemidorus, *Interpretation of Dreams* 4.30: someone "dreamed that his cloak had split in the middle. His house crumbled . . . Another who dreamed that he had lost the tile roofing of his house . . . lost his clothes."

68. For this myth see G. Dumézil, *Le crime des Lemniennes* (Paris: Geuthner, 1924); and M. Detienne, *Les jardins d'Adonis* (Paris: Gallimard, 1972), pp. 172–184; translated by J. Lloyd as *The Garden of Adonis* (Princeton: Princeton University Press, 1993).

69. Pindar, *Pythian Odes* 4.241–254. Simonides, frag. 547 *PLG* (taken from *The Scholia to Pindar*, II.160 Drachmann): "In Simonides, one also finds the story that the Argonauts competed for a garment."

70. Apollodorus, *Bibliotheca* 1.9.17.

71. Apollonius Rhodius, *Argonautica* 3.1204–06. In a different perspective from our own: A. Rose, "Clothing Imagery in Apollonius' *Argonautika*," *Quaderni Urbaniti di cultura classica*, 50 (1985), 29–44.

72. Apollonius, *Argonautica* 2.30–32. Note that the garments *worn* by Jason and Pollus cannot be *peploi* or *throna* ("flowered garments"), which are reserved for women. For the value of the *peplos* in this respect, see N. Loraux, "Le *peplos* d'Héraklès," in *Les expériences de Tirésias. Le féminin et l'homme grec* (Paris: Gallimard, 1989), pp. 153–160. The Satyrs donned *anthina himatia* for the festival of the Anthesteria: see Liddell-Scott-Jones, s.v. *anthinos*, II.

73. Pausanias 3.12.2: Apollodorus, *Bibliotheca* 2.1.5.

74. Pindar, *Pythian Odes* 9.117–120.

75. Ibid., 121–125.

76. For an analysis, see J.-P. Vernant, *Mythe et société en Grèce ancienne* (Paris: François Maspero, 1973), pp. 78–81.

77. *Od.* 19.136–161; see 2.89–110, 24.125–150.

78. Apollodorus, *Epitome* 7.38–39; Tzetzes, *The Scholia to Lycophron, Alexandra* 772. Compare Servius, *Commentary to the Aeneid* 2.44. See J. Svenbro, "Vengeance et société en Grèce archaïque," in R. Verdier et J.-P. Poly, eds., *La vengeance*, vol. 3 (Paris: Editions Cujas, 1984), pp. 52–53.

79. *Od.* 19.144–147, etc. The word *pharos* occurs in lines 138 and 142.

80. This is how V. Bérard translates (into French) 19.147, *polla kteatissas.*

81. We are borrowing this argument from R. Eisler, *Weltmantel und Himmelszelt*, vol 1 (Munich, C. H. Beck, 1910), pp. 131–132, who shares our hypothesis.

82. Artemidorus, *Interpretation of Dreams* 3.36, 4.40. See 2.49 and 65 for the analogy between marriage and death.

83. Of course, our genetic approach does not prohibit an analysis of Homer's text as we know it. Even if we see the *pharos* woven by Penelope only as a shroud, it is not devoid of conjugal symbolism, for, as Pierre Vidal-Naquet kindly pointed out to us, what is united during the day (the *stēmōn* and the *krokē*) is undone at night, which is the time of sexual union, *sumplokē* (which thus does not take place).

84. Plutarch, *Life of Romulus* 2.5.

85. Note that if she had obeyed him, the daughter of Tarchetius would have had to couple with a phallus that emerged from the hearth

of her father's home. As we have said, it is up to the "house" to furnish the wedding cloth.

86. Plutarch, *Life of Romulus* 2.6. See M. Delcourt, *Oedipe ou la légende du conquérant* (1944; reprint, Paris: Les Belles Lettres, 1981), p. 170; J. M. Moret, "Circé tisseuse sur les vases de Cabirion," *Revue archéologigue*, 2 (1991), 252, n. 175.

87. Archilochus, frag. S 478 Page. First published in R. Merkelback and M. L. West, "Ein Archilochos-Papyrus," *Zeitschrift für Papyrologie und Epigraphik*, 14 (1974), 97–113.

88. Lines 42–45.

89. Line 51.

90. For a comparable scene (though not a strictly parallel one), see Theocritus, *Idylls* 27.59–65. See also the poem by Walter de Châtillon cited by W. Theiler, "Die Uberraschung des Kölner Archilochos," *Museum Helveticum*, 34 (1977), 60 *(sub paenula = hupo chlainei)*.

91. *Anthologia Palatina* 5.165.2–5. See Chapter 1, text at note 29.

92. *Anthologia Palatina* 5.173.1–2.

93. Hesychius, s.v. *chlaina*. See Aristophanes, *Birds* 1693: *gamike chlanis*, "wedding robe."

94. *Anthologia Palatina* 5.169.3–4.

95. Plato, *Symposium* 219b–c, trans. W. Hamilton (Harmondsworth and New York: Penguin Books, 1951).

96. Athenaeus 5.219b. See [Lucian], *Amores* 49: *hupo miai chlamudi*, "beneath the same cloak" (also with respect to Alcibiades and Socrates).

97. Sappho, frag. 213.2–3 Lobel-Page. Maximus of Tyre considers the relations within the Sapphic group as analogous to those characterizing the Socratic group: to Sappho's *eros* corresponds Socrates' *erotike techne* (*Orations* 18.9 = Sappho, test. 20 Campbell). Further, if the young girl in frag. 102 Lobel-Page complains to her mother that she can no longer weave, "subjugated by the desire of [her] love, *pais* [literally 'child,' masculine or feminine]" one can imagine that the fact of interweaving warp and woof all day long suggested erotic interlacing to such an extent that "it was all she could think about." It is thus only on a superficial, practical level that weaving and love are in opposition; deep down, they are analogous.

98. Diodorus Siculus 4.39.2.

99. Pindar, *Nemean Odes* 1.37–43, trans. C. M. Bowra.

100. *Nemean Odes* 5.50.

101. For the union of Alcmena and Zeus (who takes Amphitryon's place) see notably Hesiod, *Shield of Heracles* 27–35; Apollodorus, *Bibliotheca* 2.4.8.

102. Sophocles, *The Women of Trachis.*

103. Nonnus, *Dionysiaca* 7.218.

104. Ibid., 216.

105. Ibid., 221.

106. Ibid., 282–283.

107. Ibid., 8.166.

108. Colluthus, *The Rape of Helen* 138–165, in *Oppian, Colluthus, Tryphiodorus,* trans. A. W. Mair (Cambridge, Mass.: Loeb Classical Library, Harvard University Press, 1928).

109. Ibid., 153–157.

110. Ibid., 163–164.

111. According to Pausanias 10.38.6, she is worshipped at Ephesus under a slightly different name, *Protothronie.*

112. Callimachus, *Hymn to Artemis* 225–228, in *Callimachus, Hymns and Epigrams,* trans. A. W. Mair (Cambridge, Mass.: Loeb Classical Library, Harvard University Press, 1921). Chesion and Imbrasus: headland and river in Samos.

113. We are thinking of the cultural importance of Hera in Samos, where the goddess had a famous sanctuary.

114. *Anthologia Palatina* 9.245.3.

115. Ibid.

116. *Suda,* s.v. *Arktos ē Braurōniois.*

117. Pindar, *Nemean Odes* 11.1–3.

118. Pindar, *Olympian Odes* 2.77

119. See above, text at note 24.

120. Pindar, *Olympian Odes* 14.9–11.

121. Pindar, *Nemean Odes* 10.1–2.

122. *Nemean Odes* 10.6.

123. See above, text at note 73.

124. See Chapter 1, note 123.

125. Pindar, *Nemean Odes* 10.22–23.

126. Pindar, *Olympian Odes* 2.22.

127. *Od.* 5.333–461. We owe this observation to Pierre Vidal-Naquet.

128. Pindar, *Isthmian Odes* 2.4–5, trans. C. M. Bowra.

129. Pindar, *Pythian Odes* 9.60.

130. *Pythian Odes* 9.62.

131. See above, text at note 24.

132. Pindar, *Nemean Odes* 3.83.

133. The translator of the French Belles Lettres edition leaves the epithet untranslated, perhaps for the same reason as in the note cited earlier.

134. Pindar, *Olympian Odes* 13.96.

135. Pindar, *Isthmian Odes* 6.16–17.

136. Pindar, *Nemean Odes* 4.65.

137. Hesychius, *s.v.*

138. We cite *bathupeplos* and *bussopharēs*. Like the Latin *altus*, *bathus* can mean "deep" as well as "high."

139. Pindar, *Pythian Odes* 9.68–69, trans. C. M. Bowra.

140. Ibid., 4.259–261.

141. Ibid., 3.24–27.

142. See above, text at note 36.

143. *The Scholia to Theocritus* 2.59. See above, text at note 18.

144. Although later on, in Plato (*Euthydemus* 277d), we encounter the word *thronosis,* the sense of "enthronement" is not obligatory (despite Liddel-Scott-Jones, s.v.); indeed, this meaning clashes with the fact that the *thronosis* occurs "around" *(peri)* the one who was to be initiated to the mysteries of the Corybants. As Philippe Bourgeaud kindly pointed out to us, in this passage the context is a *dance.*

145. The vestimentary rituals of this type are undoubtedly quite ancient (see J. G. Frazer, *Pausanias's Description of Greece*, vol. 3 [1898; reprint, New York: Biblio and Tannen, 1965], pp. 574–576). We may have traces of this on a Mycenean tablet published in J. Chadwick and M. Ventris, *Documents in Mycenean Greek*, 2nd ed. (Cambridge: Cambridge University Press, 1973), p. 482, no. 308: "To the two Queens on the occasion of the Thronohelkteria, sage-scented oil." We are obviously tempted to think that the Thronohelkteria were festivals on the occasion of which women wore *throna*, "flowered garments," which

they "dragged" behind them, as did the Trojans and the Lesbians qualified as *helkesipeploi*, who let "their peplos drag," in Homer and Alceus respectively (*Il.* 7.297; Alceus, frag. 130.33 Lobel-Page; cf. *helkechitones*, "who let their chitons drag," of the Ionians in *Homeric Hymn to Apollo* 147. These three examples all occur within the context of festivals; the festival in which the Lesbians *helkesipeploi* appear is a festival for Hera, according to *The Scholia to the Iliad* 9.129). But one may also imagine a peplophoria in which the flowered garments destined to cover the statues of the two goddesses are worn in such a manner that they "drag" on the ground. (For "sage-scented oil," see Chadwick and Ventris, no. 310: "Olive oil for the Mistress of *Hyp* . . . ointment for robes"). See I. K. Probonas, *Hē mukēnaikē Heortē thronoelktēpia* (Athens, 1974), for the Thronohelkteria as a festival during which one "spread" the *peplos pepoikilmenos* destined to envelop the two goddesses; P. Faure, "Crète et Mycènes: Problèmes de mythologie et d'histoire religieuse," in Y. Bonnefoy, ed., *Dictionnaire des mythologies* (Paris: Flammarion, 1981), p. 268. Our thanks to Jean-Pierre Comboul for having put us on this track.

146. A *peplophoria* would furthermore be the perfect occasion for the use of a metaphor such as *humnon huphainein*, "to weave a hymn," which we encountered in Bacchylides.

147. Orpheus, frag. A 1 Diels-Kranz.

148. Ibid.

149. See Liddell-Scott-Jones, s.v. *himatismos*.

150. See ibid., s.v.

4. The Marriage of Peleus and Thetis

1. M. Guarducci, "Il conubium nei riti del matrimonio etrusco e di quello romano," *Bullettino della commissione archeologica comunale di Roma*, 55 (1927), 205–224.

2. B.-M. Fridh-Haneson, *Le manteau symbolique: Etude sur les couples votifs en terre cuite assis sous un même manteau* (Stockholm: Paul Åströms Förlag, 1983); G. Arrigoni, "Amore sotto il manto e iniziazione nuziale," *Quaderni Urbinati di cultura classica*, 3 (1983), 7–56; H.-G. Buchholz, "Das Symbol des gemeinsamen Mantels," *Mitteilungen des*

Deutschen archäologischen Instituts. Römische Abteilung, 102 (1987), 1–55; G. Koch-Harnack, *Erotische Symbole: Lotosblüte und geinsamer Mantel auf antiken Vasen* (Berlin: Gebr. Mann Verlag, 1989), pp. 109–185.

3. G. F. Gamurrini, "Il matrimonio italico," *Mitteilungen des Deutschen archäologischen Instituts. Römische Abteilung*, 4 (1889), 89 ff.

4. Chiusi, Museo civico, no. 118 in the catalogue; drawings in Guarducci, "Il conubium," facing p. 224; and in Buchholz, "Das Symbol des gemeinsamen Mantels," p. 53.

5. For *pastos*, see Arrigoni, "Amore sotto il manto," pp. 34–41.

6. *Il.* 22.441. See Chapter 3, text at note 7.

7. Athenaeus 1.23d (= Aristotle, frag. 607 Rose); Guarducci, "Il conubium," p. 210. In our opinion, the Greek artifacts cited by Guarducci in her n. 1 should not be considered as parallel to the fragment by Aristotle, since the women who figure in them would hardly have been wives.

8. *The Scholia to Sophocles, Women of Trachis* 539: *mias hupo chlainēs: anti tou mias koitēs*. An observation quoted by Guarducci, "Il conubium," p. 223, n. 1.

9. Guarducci, "Il conubium," pp. 209–210.

10. Apollonius Rhodius, *Argonautica* 4.423–428. In our opinion, this *peplos* is not identical with the *pharos* worn by Jason, ibid., 3.1204. See Chapter 3, note 71; *contra* Arrigoni, "Amore sotto il manto," pp. 44–45, n. 89, quoting H. Shapiro, "Jason's Cloak," *Transactions and Proceedings of the American Philological Association*, 110 (1980), 271.

11. *Argonautica* 4.428–434.

12. Guarducci, "Il conubium," pp. 211–216.

13. See Pseudo-Servius, *Commentary to the Aeneid* 4.59. On the way in which weddings were performed, see J. Marquardt, *La vie privée des Romains*, vol. 1 (Paris, 1892); and L. Friedländer, *Darstellungen aus der Sittengeschichte Roms, in der Zeit von Augustus bis zum Ausgang der Antonine*, 10th ed. (1921; reprint, Darmstadt: Scientia Verlag, 1979), pp. 276 ff.

14. Guarducci, "Il conubium," pp. 214–215.

15. Ibid., p. 216 and n. 1. See A. Ernout and A. Meillet, *Dictionnaire étymologique de la langue latine*, 4th ed. (Paris: Klincksieck, 1979), p. 449, s.v. *nubo*.

16. Nonius Marcellus, *De Compendiosa Doctrina* 1, p. 208.22 Lindsay, s.v. *nubere.*

17. Guarducci, "Il conubium," p. 216 and n. 3. See Ernout and Meillet, *Dictionnaire étymologique,* pp. 448–449, s.v. *nubes* and *nubo.*

18. See Paul the Deacon, p. 201 Lindsay: *obnubit,* "she covers her head" *(caput operit).*

19. Guarducci, "Il conubium," p. 221: "Così, nel caso speciale delle nozze, il comune velo, che in origine consacrava gli sposi o un rito del matrimonio, potè in seguito esser fatto simbolo dell'unione indissolubile del marito e della moglie, o anche divenir segno della protezione che, per mezzo di matrimonio, la donna acquista da parte dell'uomo."

20. Apollonius Rhodius, *Argonautica* 3.1204–06, cited in Chapter 3, text at note 71.

21. Seneca, *Letters to Lucilius* 14.90.20. One may object that Seneca cites and translates a Greek source, which proves nothing with regard to the specifically Roman manner of conceiving of the interlacing of the threads in weaving. But a close reading of the texts tells us that Seneca criticizes Posidonius for having attributed too much importance to a vulgar manual technique, which according to the Roman has nothing to do with the philosopher (the "wise man"); in other words, Seneca finds nothing surprising or new about the Greek *sumplokē;* on the contrary, he feels almost insulted by the exegesis of something so commonplace, even *too* commonplace, by the Greek philosopher. See also Chapter 2, text at note 13, for the symbolism of interlacing in Silius Italicus.

22. Seneca, ibid., 20–21. The citation from Ovid: *Metamorphoses* 6.55–57.

23. Paul the Deacon, p. 85 Lindsay.

24. Pliny the Elder, *Natural History* 8.74 (194–195), trans. H. Rackham (Cambridge, Mass.: Loeb Classical Library, Harvard University Press, 1940).

25. For the history of Tanaquil, Servius Tullius, and the end of Roman royalty, see Livy 1.34 ff.

26. Plutarch, *On the Fortune of the Romans* 323a–d. See G. Capdeville, *Volcanus. Recherches comparatistes sur les origines du culte de*

Vulcain (Thesis under the direction of R. Bloch, University of Paris IV, 1987; for the stories of Servius Tullius, Ocrisia, etc., see pp. 8–16.

27. Plutarch, *Life of Numa* 5.1–7.1.

28. Plutarch, *Roman Questions* 30.271e, on Gaia Caecilia, which, according to Pliny the Elder, 8.194, is another name for Tanaquil.

29. Pliny the Elder, ibid.

30. Ibid., 197.

31. See Chapter 1, text at note 49.

32. See Festus, p. 198 Lindsay: Augustine, *City of God* 7.9. See also, for Jupiter's flamen, K. Latte, *Römische Religionsgeschichte*, Handbuch der Altertumswissenschaft, V.4 (Munich: C. H. Beck, 1960), pp. 402–403, etc.; G. Dumézil, *La religion romaine archaïque*, 2nd ed. (Paris: Payot, 1987), pp. 163–165.

33. Plutarch, *Roman Questions* 50.276d; see Aulus Gellius 10.15.

34. Pseudo-Servius, *Commentary to the Aeneid* 4.262.

35. For Roman woman and their work with wool, see H. Blümner, *Technologie und Terminologie der Gewerbe und Künst bei Griechen und Rümern*, vol. 1 (1912; reprint, Hildesheim: Georg Olm Verlagsbuchhandlung, 1969), pp. 104–106; also J. P. V. D. Balsdon, *Roman Women: Their History and Habits* (London: Bodley Head, 1962).

36. Varro, *De Lingua Latina* 5.132.

37. Paul the Deacon, p. 104 Lindsay.

38. Pseudo-Servius, *Commentary to the Aeneid* 4.262: *quidam muliebrem uestem quasi amatori aptam uolunt.*

39. *Aeneid* 4.166–168, trans. H. R. Fairclough.

40. Ibid., 260–264.

41. Ibid., 316.

42. Bibliography in K. Quinn, *Catullus: The Poems* (London: Macmillan, 1971), pp. 350–351; compare Arrigoni, "Amore sotto il manto," p. 18, n. 21. See also C. Calame, *Thésée et l'imaginaire athénien* (Lausanne: Payot, 1990).

43. Catullus 64.47–51.

44. Ibid., 50–264.

45. Ibid., 52–75 and 124–206.

46. Ibid., 53.

47. Ibid., 265–408.

48. Ibid., 61.

49. Ibid., 141 and 158.

50. Ibid., 69–70.

51. Pindar, *Nemean Odes* 1.37–50.

52. Ibid., 76–131.

53. Ibid., 132–201.

54. Ibid., 141.

55. *Aeneid* 4.316. Conversely, Apollo, who seeks *conubia* with Daphne (Ovid, *Metamorphoses* 1.490), is reminiscent of the god who unites with Koronis *kallipeplos* and with Cyrene *chrusothronos:* see Chapter 3, text at note 140.

56. Catullus 64.23 and 135.

57. Ibid., 159 and 151.

58. Ibid., 158–163.

59. Ibid., 49–50.

60. Ibid., 200–201.

61. Ibid., 233–237.

62. Ibid., 238–239 and 243–245.

63. Ibid., 247–248.

64. Ibid., 176.

65. Plutarch, *Life of Theseus* 19.4.

66. Ibid., 6.

67. See Catullus 64.85–87 and 176.

68. Ibid., 113.

69. Apollodorus, *Epitome* 1.8–9.

70. Pherekydes, cited in *The Scholia to the Odyssey* 11.320 (= *FGrHist* 3 F 148); Propertius 4.4.42. See Chapter 2, note 29 and accompanying text.

71. Catullus 64.149; in spinning, the *turbo* is the rotating element thanks to which the spindle is held in balance: ibid., 314 (see Blümner, *Technologie und Terminologie der Gewerbe*, p. 124).

72. Apollodorus, *Epitome* 1.14; see *Anthologia Palatina* 6.24.1; Hesychius and the *Suda*, s.v. *laburinthos: kochlioeides topos.* See M. Detienne, *L'écriture d'Orphée* (Paris: Gallimard, 1989), pp. 24–25.

73. For this expression, see Catullus 64.334: *domus . . . contexit amores.*

74. F. Frontisi-Ducroux, *Dédale: Mythologie de l'artisan en Grèce ancienne* (Paris: François Maspero, 1975), p. 143: "By every indication, it is a symbolic form, with no architectural referent."

75. *Aeneid* 5.588–593, trans. H. R. Fairclough. See Chapter 2.

76. Plutarch, *Life of Theseus* 21.1–2 (right horns according to the same Plutarch, *The Cleverness of Animals* 983e). For the Keraton, see W. Deonna, "Les cornes gauches," *Revue des études anciennes,* 42 (1940), 111–126; P. Bruneau, *Recherches sur les cultes de Délos à l'époque hellénistique et à l'époque impériale* (Paris: De Boccard, 1970), pp. 19–35; also F. Williams, *Callimachus, Hymn to Apollo: A Commentary* (Oxford: Clarendon Press, 1978), pp. 59–60.

77. *The Scholia to the Iliad* 18.590.

78. Ibid.: *khoron toiouton epleken . . .* We know that *plekein* is used in the sense of "weaving" in Plato and in Theocritus (see Chapter 5, note 26).

79. Philostratus, *Heroicus* 11.4.

80. "And Theseus led the chorus," writes Callimachus, *Hymn to Delos* 313, which means that he was the first *Geranoulkos,* the term for the person who trails, or rather leads, the "Crane" (Hesychius, s.v.). The second element of this choreographic term is derived from the verb *helkein,* "to trail," which also comes into play in the word *thronohelktēria* mentioned earlier (Chapter 3, note 145).

81. Eustathius, *Commentary to the Iliad* 18. 590, cited by Frontisi-Ducroux, *Dédale,* p. 145 and n. 54. See Lucian, *On Dance* 11–12, on the subject of the dance called the "Necklace" *(hormos),* interlacing *(plekein)* the "modesty" of the girls and the "courage" of the boys.

82. Aristotle, *History of Animals* 597a30–31: cranes fly "from one extremity of the world to the other."

83. This is how we understand the word *parallaxeis* in Plutarch, *Life of Theseus* 21.1.

84. Callimachus, *Hymn to Apollo* 60–64. According to line 61, Apollo "wove" *(epleke)* the alter of horns (see *huphainei,* line 57, for the meaning): Plutarch is thus right to compare the nest "woven" by

the halcyon with the altar "woven" by Apollo (*The Cleverness of Animals* 983c–e).

85. Plutarch, *Life of Theseus* 24.1–3.

86. Catullus 64.132–201.

87. Ibid., 261.

88. Ibid., 264.

89. Ibid.

90. Ibid., 267–304.

91. Ibid., 305–383.

92. Ibid., 298.

93. Ibid., 292–293.

94. Ibid., 334–335.

95. Pindar, *Pythian Odes* 3.90.

96. Catullus 64.311–314 and 320–322.

97. Ibid., 338–370. See Appendix A.

98. Catullus 64.372–380.

99. Ibid., 384–385.

100. Ibid., 395–397.

101. Ibid., 399–406.

102. Hermogenes, "On the Ekphrasis," p. 23 Rabe (in *Rhetores Graeci*, VI, *Hermogenis Opera* [Leipzig, 1913]).

103. We will survey *textus* and *texere* in detail later.

104. Plutarch, *Advice to Bride and Groom* 138b, in *Moralia*, trans. Harold Cherniss (Cambridge, Mass.: Loeb Classical Library, Harvard University Press, 1957).

105. Ibid., 138c.

5. *The Cloak of Phaedrus*

1. See, for example, D. Dubuisson, "Anthropologie poétique: Prolégomènes à une anthropolgie du texte," *L'homme*, 111–112 (1989), 222–236; M. Durante, "Ricerche sulla preistoria della lingua poetica greca: La terminologia relativa alla creazione poetica," *Rendiconti della classe di scienze morali, storiche e filologiche dell'Accademia dei Linci*, 15 (1960), 231–149; also R. Schmitt, *Dichtung und Dichtersprache in indogermanischer Zeit* (Wiesbaden: Harrassowitz, 1967), pp. 300–301. For

the metaphor of language weaving outside the Indo-European domain, see—also as an example—P. Galand-Pernet, "Littérature orale et représentation du texte: Les poèmes berbères traditionnels," *Etudes de littérature ancienne*, 3 ("Le texte et ses représentations") (1987), 112 and n. 13 (with bibliographical information).

2. Consider, for instance, the opening pages of J. Derrida, "La pharmacie de Platon," in *La dissémination* (Paris: Editions du Minuit, 1972), pp. 71–74.

3. The term *rhapsōidos* appears for the first time in Herodotus 5.67 in connection with rhapsodic competitions in Sicyon shortly before 600 B.C. See J. Svenbro, *La parole et le marbre: Aux origines de la poétique grecque* (Thesis, Lund, 1976), pp. 44–45. The best-known rhapsodist is obviously Ion, the protagonist of the Platonic dialogue that bears his name.

4. The formula is found in [Hesiod], frag. 357 Merkelbach-West, portraying Hesiod and Homer as old colleagues in Delos. See Svenbro, *La parole*, pp. 201–202.

5. The text on which V. Bérard bases his French translation of *Odyssey* 8.499, "l'aède . . . leur tissait son hymne" (the bard wove his hymn for them) is the translator's own creation.

6. See Svenbro, *La parole*, pp. 200–204: in particular, with expressions such as *metin huphainein* and *kaka rhaptein*.

7. *Il.* 3.207–223; translation based on Richmond Lattimore's.

8. In the *Odyssey*, it is the bard of the Phaeacians, Demodocus, who receives the Muse's song (8.64, 73, 499); in the *Iliad*, it is Homer himself who asks for the Muse's assistance for his own song (2.484–493).

9. *Il.* 2.594–600. See Svenbro, *La parole*, p. 24 and passim.

10. Similarly, the art of archery is not the private property of the archer, as shown in the story of Eurytos, who competed with the Archer himself, Apollo. Furious, the latter killed him (*Od.* 8.223–228).

11. See Svenbro, *La parole*, pp. 16–45; cf. pp. 162–163.

12. *Il.* 3.150–155, trans. Lattimore.

13. This in effect is how Frontisi-Ducroux understands Helen's weaving, who is defined as "a hypostasis of the poet" (*La cithare d'Achille: Essai sur la poétique de l'Iliade* [Rome: Edizioni dell'Ateneo,

1986], p. 49 and n. 166). See also A. Bergren, "Language and the Female in Early Greek Thought," *Arethusa*, 16 (1983), 70–75 (as well as Dubuisson, "Anthropologie poétique," p. 223).

14. Plato, *Euthyphro* 6b–c.

15. *Od.* 5.58–62, trans. G. H. Palmer.

16. *Od.* 10.221–223.

17. J. McIntosh Snyder, "The Web of Song," *Classical Journal*, 76 (1981), 194.

18. Pindar, *Nemean Odes* 4.44–46.

19. This observation was made by Snyder, "The Web of Song," pp. 194–195; compare *Anthologia Palatina* 2.395–397 on Alcman (a reference we owe to Peter J. Wilson). For poetry and the craft of weaving, see B. Gallet, *Recherches sur kairos et l'ambiguïté dans la poésie de Pindare* (Bordeaux: Presses Universitaires de Bordeaux, 1990) (a reference we owe to Claude Calame); for a critique, see M. Trédé, *Kairos: L'à-propos et l'occasion*, Etudes et Commentaires, 103 (Paris: Klincksieck, 1992), pp. 73–76. Providing the background to this debate on *kairos* is R. B. Onians, *The Origins of European Thought*, 2nd ed. (Cambridge: Cambridge University Press, 1954), pp. 343–351.

20. For example, in *Anthologia Palatina* 6.83.5: *kitharēs mitos*.

21. Alcman, frag. 1.67–68 Page; Sappho, frag. 98a.10, 98b.3 Lobel-Page: *mitrana* = *mitra*.

22. Pindar, *Nemean Odes* 8.15.

23. Ibid., 14–16; *The Scholia to Pindar*, III.142.12–16 Drachmann.

24. Pindar, frag. 169 Bowra.

25. Pindar, *Olympian Odes* 6.85–87.

26. Plato, *Statesman* 283a *(plekein);* Theocritus, *Idylls* 18.34 *(sumplekein)*. *Plekein* is used instead of *huphainein* when one wishes to emphasize the aspect of interweaving. For *poikilon*, see Liddell-Scott-Jones, s.v. *poikilos*, II.1; cf. s.v. *poikillo*, I, as well as *poikilma*, I.

27. Bacchylides, *Victory Odes* 5.8–14.

28. For the hypothesis of an etymological link between *huphainein* and *humnos*, see, for example, R. Eisler, *Welmantel und Himmelszelt*, vol. 1 (Munich: C. H. Beck, 1910), pp. 110 and 130–131, n. 2. See P. Chantraine, *Dictionnaire étymologique de la langue grecque* (Paris: Klincksieck, 1968–1980), p. 1156, who is decidedly skeptical.

29. Bacchylides, *Victory Odes* 5.11.

30. Bacchylides, *Dithyrambs* 19(= 5 Irigoin).8–11. A contemporary of the choral poets (and undoubtedly attentive to their jargon), Epicharmus (frag. B 6 Diels-Kranz) uses the same metaphor: one day, he says, someone will "remove [*periduein*] the metric form" of his work in order to "give [it] a purple garment [*heima*], having embroidered [*poikillein*] it with beautiful words."

31. Snyder, "The Web of Song," p. 194: "Thus, while Homer himself never actually describes poetic activity as analogous to weaving at the loom, his frequent references to metaphorical and literal weaving, as well as his juxtaposition of actual weaving and singing, lay the foundation for the lyric poets' description of their own webs of song."

32. Here we essentially follow the analysis proposed in Svenbro, *La parole*, pp. 5–6, 162–212.

33. Aristotle, *Rhetoric* 3.2.1405b23–28.

34. Svenbro, *La parole*, pp. 172–186.

35. Ibid., pp. 16–35.

36. See ibid., pp. 141–161.

37. See M. Detienne, *Les maîtres de vérité dans la Grèce archaïque* (Paris: François Maspero, 1967), pp. 81–103.

38. Svenbro, *La parole*, pp. 5–6 and 205–212.

39. Henceforth, Homer is "*the* Poet," *ho poiētēs*, for the Greeks: see Liddell-Scott-Jones, s.v. *poiētēs*, II (with references). By being referred to in this way, he was attributed with a blasphemy of which he never proved guilty: for him, the bard "produces" nothing; he "receives" his words from the Muse.

40. Plato, *Protagoras* 316d. As opposed to a Homer or a Hesiod (also mentioned here), Simonides (who died in 476 B.C.) is relatively close in time to Protagoras (who was born in about 485).

41. See P. Vidal-Naquet, *Le chasseur noir* (Paris: François Maspero, 1981), p. 308; translated by Andrew Szegedy-Maszak as *The Black Hunter* (Baltimore: Johns Hopkins University Press, 1986).

42. Plato, *Statesman* 277d.

43. Ibid., 278b.

44. Plato, *Sophist* 262b–e; see also 259e.

45. It must be emphasized that "harmony" can be established only

between two dissimilar things: "What is similar [*homoia*] and related [*homophula*] needs no harmony [*harmonia*]," says Philolaos, frag. B 6 Diels-Kranz.

46. Plato, *Symposium* 219b–c.

47. The analysis proposed here takes as its starting point that found in J. Svenbro, *Phrasikleia: An Anthropology of Reading in Ancient Greek*, trans. J. Lloyd (Ithaca: Cornell University Press, 1993), pp. 198–216.

48. Plato, *Phaedrus* 229a–234b. The fact that the plane tree beneath which the reading takes place is next to the Ilissos River is not without significance: the name *Ilissos* easily evokes a Greek verb meaning "to read," namely *(an-)elissein*, literally "to unfold" (Xenophon, *Memorabilia* 1.6.14; Straton, *Anthologia Palatina* 12.208.4).

49. We are thinking mainly of the Doric epigram of Gela, dating from 500–480 B.C.: see B. Forssman, "ANNEMOTA in einer dorischen Geffässinschrift," *Münchener Studien zur Sprachwissenschaft*, 34 (1976), 39–44; as well as C. Gallavotti, "Letture epigrafiche," *Quaderni Urbanati di cultura classica*, 20 (1975), 172–175; and the analyses of Svenbro, *Phrasikleia*, pp. 189–198.

50. Plato, *Phaedrus* 228e, trans. R. Hackforth (Cambridge: Cambridge University Press, 1972).

51. Ibid., 228d.

52. See primarily P. Chantraine, "Les verbes grecs signifiant 'lire' . . .," in *Mélanges Grégoire*, vol. 2 (Brussels: Institut de philologie et d'histoire orientales, 1950), pp. 122–126 (*entunchanein:* Longinus, *On the Sublime* 1.1, etc.) and 118 (*sungignesthai:* Gregory of Nazianzus 6.18 [vol. 1, col. 745 Migne]). For the same two verbs in the sexual sense, see Plutarch, *Life of Solon* 20.4; Xenophon, *Anabasis* 1.2.12, etc.

53. See Svenbro, *Phrasikleia*, pp. 45, 62–63, and 164.

54. On silent reading, see ibid., pp. 160–186; idem, "La Grèce archaïque et classique: L'invention de la lecture silencieuse," in G. Cavallo and R. Chartier, eds., *Histoire de la lecture dans le monde occidental: Normes et pratiques* (Paris: Editions du Seuil-Laterza, forthcoming).

55. Euripides, *Hippolytus* 865, 877, 879–880; for an analysis, see Svenbro, *Phrasikleia*, pp. 178–179.

56. *Anthologia Palatina* 9.372. We are returning here to the analysis

proposed in J. Svenbro, "La cigale et les fourmis: Voix et écriture dans une allégorie grecque," *Opuscula Romana*, 18 (1990), 18. For the date of the epigram, see D. L. Page, *Further Greek Epigrams* (Cambridge: Cambridge University Press, 1981), p. 550: "This epigram . . . contains nothing incompatible with a date in the Hellenistic or early Imperial period."

57. Democritus, frag. B 154 Diels-Kranz. See the juxtaposition of the spider and the weaver in Hesiod, *Works and Days* 777–779.

58. For *huphos*, see, for example, Plutarch, *The Oracles at Delphi* 396b ("fabric"); Longinus, *On the Sublime* 1.4 ("text"). We discuss *textus* at greater length in the next chapter.

59. It is by ellipsis that the text of the epigram merely says *lepton:* we are following Page, *Further Greek Epigrams*, p. 551, who, following J. F. Dübner, understands *lepton* in the sense of *lepton huphasma* (= *lepton huphos*), the noun being suggested by the participle *huphenamena*, which follows *lepton*. See also Dioscorides 2.63 (*huphos* in the sense of "spider's web").

60. For a more extensive argument, see Svenbro, "La Grèce archaïque et classique," especially pp. 8–16.

61. See Chantraine, "Les verbes grecs signifiant 'lire' . . .," p. 1110, who, following L. Gil Fernández, considers *tettix* to be derived from *tittix*.

62. Aesop, fable 298 Hausrath-Hunger (*Corpus Fabularum Aesopicarum*, I.2, pp. 107–108).

63. See, for example, *Anacreontea*, 32 Bergk³.

64. Lucian, *Pseudologist* 1; Plato, *Phaedrus* 259b–c.

65. See Chantraine, "Les verbes grecs signifiant 'lire' . . .," p. 622, s.v. *lasko*.

66. Aelian, *Nature of Animals* 6.57.

67. Plutarch, *The Cleverness of Animals* 966e–f.

68. Plato, *Statesman* 283b; see Philolaos, cited above, note 45.

6. The Birth of an Ideogram

1. Ovid, *Metaphorphoses* 6.1–145. I. Papdopoulou-Belmehdi, *L'art de Pandora: La mythologie du tissage en Grèce ancienne* (Thesis under

the direction of N. Loraux, Ecole des Hautes Etudes en Sciences Sociales, Paris, 1992), p. 303, draws our attention to another version of the story: see *The Scholia to Nicander, Thariaca* 12a, p. 40 Crugnola (which tells of an Athenian Arachne, a weaver whose brother, a warrior, is named Phalanx); see P. M. C. Forbes Irving, *Metamorphosis in Greek Myths* (Oxford: Clarendon Press, 1990), pp. 308–309. Compare Chapter 1, note 38.

2. Plato, *Phaedrus* 259b–c (= Aesop, fable 399 Halm).

3. Ovid, *Metamorphoses* 6.6: *lanificae non cedere laudibus artis.*

4. *Il.* 2.594–600.

5. Ovid, *Metamorphoses* 6.136–145.

6. Ibid., 5.250–678. It is during Minerva's visit to the Muses that one of the latter recounts the competition between the Muses and the Pierides.

7. Ibid., 308–310.

8. Ibid., 318–331.

9. Ibid., 341–664.

10. Ibid., 664–678.

11. Ibid., 6.4.

12. Ibid., 5–145.

13. See P. Chantraine, *Dictionnaire étymologique de la langue grecque* (Paris: Klincksieck, 1968–1980), p. 779 (s.v. *oida*, B).

14. Ovid, *Metamorphoses* 6.18.

15. Ibid., 23–25.

16. Ibid., 42.

17. Ibid., 70–102.

18. Ibid., 103–128.

19. Ibid., 129–145.

20. Ibid., 5.325–328.

21. Ibid., 6.103–107.

22. Plutarch, *On the Fame of the Athenians* 246f, etc.

23. *Il.* 3.125–138.

24. *Il.* 2.594–600.

25. [Virgil], *Culex* 2: *atque ut araneoli tenuem formauimus orsum.* See R. S. Radford, "The *Culex* and Ovid," *Philologus*, 40 (1931), 68–117.

26. Catullus 64.397–408.

27. Longinus, *On the Sublime* 17.1.

28. See the edition of R. O. A. M. Lyne, *Ciris: A Poem Attributed to Virgil* (Cambridge: Cambridge University Press, 1978), in particular pp. 108 ff.

29. "To cut" in Greek is *keirien*, which is a first element for the interpretation of the metamorphosis of Scylla into a *keiris*. See Ovid, *Metamorphoses* 8.150–151: "She takes the name *ciris*, which recalls the hair she cut."

30. *Ciris* 414–415.

31. For the story of Scylla's betrayal, see Apollodorus, *Bibliotheca* 3.15.8 (with references given ad loc. by J. G. Frazer in the Loeb edition).

32. *Ciris* 42–45.

33. Hesychius, s.v. *keiris*.

34. Alcman, frag. 26.4 Page.

35. *Ciris* 2.

36. Aristophanes, *Birds* 299–300. See Hesychius, s.v. *keirulos*.

37. *Anthologia Palatina* 6.160.

38. Euripides, frag. 523 Nauck²; Aristophanes, *Frogs* 1315–16. See H. Blümner, *Technologie und Terminologie der Gewerbe und Künste bei Griechen und Römern*, vol. 1 (1912; reprint, Hildesheim: Georg Olms Verlagsbuchhandlung, 1969), p. 151 and n. 9.

39. Aelian, *Nature of Animals* 9.17: "It looks like a woman skillful at weaving [*huphantikē*] in the process of interlacing [*epiplekein*] the warp [*stēmōn*] and the woof [*krokē*]," he says, describing the way the halcyon builds its nest (in the same passage we find the terms *sumplekein*, *plegma*, *exuphainein*, *harmozein*, and *dihuphainein*). We have already pointed out that for Plutarch (*The Cleverness of Animals* 983c–e, with *enkataplekein*, *stēmōn*, and *krokē*) the halcyon's "woven" nest is reminiscent of the altar of horns, the Keraton, in Delos, which is also "woven" (Callimachus, *Hymn to Apollo* 61: *epleke*; compare 57: *huphainei*).

40. *Ciris* 9.

41. Ibid., 14.

42. Ibid., 16–20.

43. Ibid., 21.

44. Ibid., 22–23.

45. Ibid., 29.

46. Ibid., 39. Compare Tibullus, *Panegyric to Messalla* 5–6: *chartis intexere . . . facta,* "to weave your actions into a book."

47. *Ciris* 36–41. See Appendix B.

48. See Chapter 5, text at note 34.

49. *Ciris* 100.

50. Cicero, *Letters to His Friends* 9.21.1.

51. *Letters to Quintus* 3.5. The French translator of this letter for the Collection des Universités de France edition, L.-A. Constans, pointlessly flattens the image implied by *sane texebatur opus,* translating it as "the writing [of the work] was going very well." The work to which Cicero is referring is *De Republica,* as if Cicero had in mind Plato's weaver king.

52. See Blümner, *Technologie und Terminologie,* pp. 146–147, who points out that Latin has no term corresponding to the Greek *laiai.*

53. *Laws* 1.3.9.

54. Cicero, *Pro Caelio* 8.18.

55. An important article on this subject is P. Veyne, "L'hellénisation de Rome et la problématique des acculturations," *Diogène,* 106 (April–June 1979), 3–29.

56. A perceptive article by A. Deremetz, "Le *carmen deductum* ou le fil du poème: A propos de Virgile, *Buc.,* VI," *Latomus,* 46 (1987), 762–777, is situated within this perspective.

57. Bacchylides, *Victory Odes* 5.8–14.

58. See J. Svenbro, *Phrasikleia: An Anthropology of Reading in Ancient Greece,* trans. J. Lloyd (Ithaca: Cornell University Press, 1993), pp. 109–116, citing A. Magdelain, *La loi à Rome* (Paris: Les Belles Lettres, 1978), p. 17.

59. Pliny the Elder, *Natural History* 13.21.69.

60. Ibid., 68.

61. Ibid., 27.84.

62. Ibid., 22.72.

63. This is the word that the author of the *Ciris* uses to qualify his "woven" poem (line 39); see also Tibullus, *Panegyric to Messalla* 5, cited above, note 46.

64. Pliny the Elder, *Natural History* 13.23.74.

65. Ibid., 77.

66. Ibid., 24.79.

67. Ibid., 26.83.

68. Verb: *exhegeisthai.* Cf. Svenbro, *Phrasikleia,* pp. 117–122.

69. Phlegon of Tralles, *FGrHist,* 257 F 36.10. The word *histos* appears first in line (A) 2, then in lines (A) 8, 20, (B) 30 and 34; see also (B) 65: *kerkis,* "shuttle." For a commentary on the whole, see H. Diels, *Sibyllinische Blätter* (Berlin: Georg Reimer, 1890).

70. Dionysius of Halicarnassus 4.62.5–6. For acrostic poetry see, for example, F. Dornseiff, *Das Alphabet in Mystik und Magie,* 2nd ed. (Leipzig: Teubner, 1925).

71. See Cicero, *On Divination* 2.54.112: *carmen omne praetexitur,* in which the last word evokes the *toga praetexta,* thus possessing a connotation of important public responsibility (magistrates and priests wear pretext togas). If the acrostic is a "pretext," it confers on the oracle a status of great importance.

72. Ibid., 110–112. See J. Scheid, "La parole des dieux: L'originalité du dialogue des Romains avec leurs dieux," *Opus,* 608 (1987–1989), 125–136.

73. We are thinking in particular of lines (A) 27–28 and (B) 36.

74. For the construction of oracles, see Ammianus Marcellinus 29.1.24–32; Apuleius, *Metamorphoses* 9.8. See also *Life of Aesop* (G, W, and L) 78, pp. 60, 97, and 128–129 Perry, an account we found highly instructive, even though the procedure described does not concern the construction of a versified oracle.

75. Phlegon of Tralles, *FGrHist,* 257 F 36.10, (A) 16.

76. See Chapter 5.

77. *Anthologia Latina,* no. 721.

78. Luxurius, *Poems,* no. 288 Happ.

79. Our source for Luxurius is H. Happ, *Luxurius,* vol. 1: *Text und Untersuchungen;* vol. 2: *Kommentar* (Stuttgart: Teubner, 1986); we should particularly cite vol. 1, pp. 83–91 ("Leben und Person des Luxurius").

80. See Chapter 5, text at note 61.

81. See Happ, *Luxurius,* vol. 2, pp. 34–36.

82. Ibid., p. 33: "Der allgemeine Sinn ist klar: Wo du doch ältere Autoren hast, die du billigen kannst, warum *liest* du da mich?" (italics added). Happ, however, does not draw the obvious conclusion (p. 34): "Was retexis hier heissen soll, ist völlig unklar: Rosenblum [M. Rosenblum, *Luxorius*, New York: Columbia University Press, 1961] stellt 'read, open, turn to' zur Wahl, aber für keine der Bedeutungen gibt es Parallelen." Yet see Apuleius, *Metamorphoses* 9.17.2; Symmachus, *Letters* 1.37.2; also Horace, *Satires* 2.3.2: *retexens*, which one could perfectly translate as "reading" (even though this does not conform to the usual interpretation of the passage).

83. Quintilian, *Institutio Oratoria* 9.4.13.

84. Ibid., 17.

85. By "Longinus" we mean the anonymous author of the treatise, which was probably written during the first century. For the date, we are relying on the introduction of W. Rhys Roberts' edition, *Longinus on the Sublime* (Cambridge: Cambridge University Press, 1935).

86. Longinus, *On the Sublime* 1.4. Among the uses of *huphos* = *textus*, we should mention Galen 17.1.80 Kühn (second century). Galen in fact uses *plokē* in the sense of "histological structure" (*De usu partium* 1.9 Helmreich); see Appendix A.

87. See G. Genette, *Mimologiques: Voyage en Cratylie* (Paris: Editions du Seuil, 1976).

88. See C. Lévi-Strauss, *Anthropologie structurale* (Paris: Plon, 1958), pp. 103–108, especially p. 105: "This *a posteriori* determination occurs on two levels: that of phonetics and that of vocabulary." A third should be added: the level of the graphic form (see Genette, *Mimologiques*, pp. 71–81).

Appendix A. Note on Biological "Tissue"

1. Psalms 139:13.

2. Leucippus, frag. A 15 Diels-Kranz. "To be conceived or engendered" is our translation of *gennasthai*. We should emphasize that the context of the fragment is cosmological rather than biological. In this appendix we are dealing with the "microcosm," as J.-M. Moret would

say ("Circé tisseuse sur les vases de Cabirion," *Revue archéologique*, 2 [1991], 248); we return to the "macrocosm" in Appendix B.

3. Catullus 64.326–327: *Sed uos, quae fata secuntur, / currite ducentes subtegmina, currite fusi* (But run ye on, drawing the woof threads that the Fates follow, ye spindles, run). Line 327 constitutes the refrain of the Fates repeated twelve times.

4. Horace, *Epodes* 13.15–16: *reditum certo subtemine Parcae / rupere*.

5. *Stamina ruperunt subito tua candida Parcae (Corpus Inscriptionum Latinarum*, VI.25063.17, quoted by R. B. Onians, *The Origins of European Thought*, 2nd ed. [Cambridge: Cambridge University Press, 1954], p. 350). Compare Seneca, *Apocolocyntosis* 4: *stamina . . . abrupit*.

6. This is all the more suggestive because there is an analogy between the shuttle and the arrow: see Onians, *Origins of European Thought*, pp. 343–348.

7. Ibid., pp. 349–351, citing the anonymous lyrical frag. 5 Diehl (p. 349 and n. 1; cf. p. 417).

8. Artemidorus, *Interpretation of Dreams* 3.36, 4.40.

9. Herodotus 2.123.

10. Xenophanes, frag. B 7 Diels-Kranz.

11. Aristotle, *On the Soul* 407b21–23, trans. W. S. Hett (Cambridge, Mass.: Loeb Classical Library, Harvard University Press, 1936).

12. Pindar, *Olympian Odes* 2.55–77; frag. 127 Bowra. Although the idea expressed in Orpheus, frag. 10 a Diels-Kranz, is close to the theme studied here (the formation of the body's organs is compared to the braiding of a net), we do not think it is a matter here of metaphorical *weaving*.

13. *The Republic of Plato*, 620c, trans. F. M. Cornford (Oxford: Oxford University Press, 1945).

14. For example, in Euripides, *Bacchae* 853: *endusetai stolen*.

15. Empedocles, frag. B 117 Diels-Kranz (he was a boy, a girl, a bush, a bird, and a fish).

16. Empedocles, frag. B 126 Diels-Kranz. See R. Eisler, *Himmelszelt und Welmantel*, vol. 1 (Munich: C. H. Beck, 1910), p. 243 n. 3 (a note to which we are much indebted).

17. The word *chitōn* would experience a certain success in physiological vocabulary: see Liddell-Scott-Jones, s.v. *chitōn*, IV, 1; Moret,

"Circé tisseuse," p. 248, n. 129. Might this "success" be due to the fact that the word, written in Greek letters, contains an X (XITΩN)? See Chapter 6.

18. See Heraclitus, frag. B 40 Diels-Kranz.

19. For the weaving of the spider, see Chapter 5.

20. Heraclitus, frag. B 67 a Diels-Kranz.

21. Plato, *Phaedo* 87b–88b.

22. Plato, *Gorgias* 523c–e.

23. Plato, *Timaeus* 41d.

24. Ibid., 72c. The reader who wishes to pursue this line of inquiry will find elements in G. Zuntz, *Persephone* (Oxford: Clarendon Press, 1971), pp. 405–406, as well as in Moret, "Circé tisseuse," notably p. 248 and n. 129.

Appendix B. Note on Cosmic "Weaving"

1. See Chapter 6.

2. [Virgil], *Ciris* 36–41. Line 39 *(naturae rerum magnis intexere chartis)* has a perceptible Lucretian resonance (*De rerum natura* 4.969–970: *naturam quaerere rerum . . . patriis exponere chartis*).

3. Lucretius, *De rerum natura* 5.1350–1360, trans. Cyril Bailey (Oxford: Clarendon Press, 1947).

4. On the other hand, one encounters *retexere* in the sense of "undoing the fabric": ibid., 1.529, 267, 389. In a cosmology which, like that of Empedocles, contracts Venus and Mars as Union and Separation, *retexere* would obviously fall into the category of Mars (present in the prologue, 1.32; compare 5.1304).

5. See first of all the index of Diels-Kranz, s.v. *sumplekein* and *sumplokē*. For the theme of the "cosmic fabric" in general, we can cite the rich—probably overly rich—work by R. Eisler, *Himmelszelt und Weltmantel*, 2 vols. (Munich: C. H. Beck, 1910).

6. *Textum: De rerum natura* 5.94, 351; 6.997, 1054; *textura:* 1.247 (cf. 3.209); 4.158, 196, 657; 6.776, 1084; *textus:* 4.728. We are borrowing the expression "atomic structure" from the second edition of C. Bailey's classic *Titi Lucreti Cari De rerum natura*, 3 vols. (Oxford: Clarendon Press, 1950; cited hereafter as Bailey).

7. See G. A. Ferrari, "La scrittura fine della realtà," in F. Romano, ed., *Democrito e l'atomismo antico*, Siculorum Gymnasium, 33 (Catania, 1980), pp. 75–89; H. Wismann, "Réalité et matière dans l'atomisme démocritéen," ibid., pp. 61–74.

8. See especially *De rerum natura* 1.817–829. "Tragedy and Comedy are written with the same letters," we read in the atomist Leucippus; similarly, in the physical world, it is the same "letters" that combine and recombine to create the diversity of things (Leucippus, frag. A 9 Diels-Kranz). See J. Svenbro, *Phrasikleia: An Anthropology of Reading in Ancient Greece*, trans. J. Lloyd (Ithaca: Cornell University Press, 1993), pp. 174–176; and especially M. Bollack, *La raison de Lucrèce: Constitution d'une poétique philosophique, avec un essai d'interprétation de la critique lucrétienne* (Paris: Editions du Minuit, 1978).

9. See Chapter 4.

10. For the distinction *grammata/stoicheia*, see Liddell-Scott-Jones, s.v. *stoicheion*, II, 1; cf. J. Svenbro, "La cigale et les formis: Voix et écriture dans une allégorie grecque," *Opuscula Romana*, 18 (1990), 16 and n. 87; idem, "La Grèce archaïque et classique: l'invention de la lecture silencieuse," in G. Cavallo and R. Chartier, eds., *Histoire de la lecture dans le monde occidental. Normes et pratiques* (Paris: Editions du Seuil-Laterza, forthcoming).

11. See Bailey, vol. 3, pp. 66–72.

12. See ibid., vol. 1, pp. 69–70.

13. *De rerum natura* 1.1.

14. For the *intermundia* (in Greek: *metakosmia*), see Bailey, vol. 1, p. 69.

15. For a critical panorama of interpretations, see Bailey, vol. 2, pp. 589–591. See also the rich book by R. Schilling, *La religion romaine de Vénus depuis les origines jusqu'au temps d'Auguste* (Paris: De Boccard, 1954), pp. 346–358; P. Grimal, "Lucrèce et l'hymne à Vénus: Essai d'interprétation," *Revue des études latines*, 35 (1957), 184–195; and C. Salemme, "L'inno a Venere di Lucrezio," *Bollettino di studi latini*, 7 (1977), 3–24.

16. These are the "three great 'texts'" of the universe, the *tria talia texta* of *De rerum natura* 5.94.

17. Ibid., 1.21–28. We should point out that poetic composition is

understood here as the passage from the oral *(dicere)* to the written *(scribere)*.

18. Ibid., 921–950.

19. Plutarch, *Advice to Bride and Groom,* 138c–d.

20. Sappho, frag. 1.28 Lobel-Page: *summachos.* Lucretius imitator of Sappho, frag. 31 Lobel-Page: *De rerum natura* 3.154–156.

21. *Homeric Hymn to Aphrodite* 5.1–5.

22. We are not insisting on the epithet, but see Bailey, vol. 2, pp. 589–591.

23. L. Kahn, *Hermès passe, ou les ambiguïtés de la communication* (Paris: François Maspero, 1978), p. 170.

INDEX

Civitalba, 85, 87
Claudius, 41, 147
Clio, 78, 79
Clotho, 79
Clouds, The (Aristophanes), 21
Colluthus, 74
Coronis, 80
"Crane," 102–103
Crassus, Marcus Licinius, 143
Cratylists, 155
Crete, 43, 97, 98, 101
Culex, 136–137
Customs of the Tyrrhenians (Aristotle), 85
Cypria, 57–58
Cypriots, 55
Cypris, 71, 74
Cyrene, 78, 79, 80

Daedalus, 44, 99–100, 102
Damophon, 10
Danaids, 77, 79
Danaus, 67, 68, 77
Darwinism, 155
David, 157
Dawn, 59–60
Deianeira, 73
Deinias of Aegina, 117
Delos/Delians, 101, 102, 103
Demeter, 36, 37
Demiurge, 162
Demo, 71
Democritus, 128, 166
Demosthenes, 153
De rerum natura (Lucretius), 165, 167–169
Detienne, Marcel, 4
Deucalion, 14
Dia, 96, 97, 104

Diana. *See* Artemis/Diana
Dicaearchus, 102
Dido, 90, 94–95, 97, 99
Diels, Hermann, 40
Diodorus Siculus, 56
Diomedes, 17
Dionysiaca (Nonnus), 74
Dionysos/Bacchus, 74, 85, 86, 88, 104, 132, 134
Drusilla, 41

Egypt/Egyptians, 132, 146, 160
Elea, 34
Elean festival, 12–13
Eleans, 10, 34, 61, 82
Elis, 10–11, 12, 14, 15, 17, 18, 22, 31, 32, 33, 34, 34, 81, 82, 92
Empedocles, 161
Endumatia, 31, 77
Endymion, 14–15, 34, 70–71, 161
Enthronismoi (Pindar), 81–82
Envy, 134
Enyalius, 74
"Epithalamium of Helen" (Theocritus), 62
Erechtheum, 18
Erechtheus, 140
Ergastinai, 18
Eros, 65
Etruscans, 85, 88
Euclid, 130
Eudumatia, 161
Eumaeus, 58
Eumenides, 98
Euneos, 67
Euripides, 63, 127
Europe, 134
Eurydice, 107
Eurylochus, 117

REVEALING ANTIQUITY

G. W. Bowersock, General Editor